Pray Every Day

Phyllis Joan Atkins
Confirmed 25 11 77

FAITH

FURNISHES PRAYER
with wings, without
which it cannot soar to

HEAVEN.

S. John Climacus.

Copyright Elizabeth Griffiths No. 45

Pray Every Day

Readings, Poems and Prayers
for every day of the year

*Ronald Jasper, Peter Coughlan
and David Jasper*

COLLINS

Collins Liturgical Publications
187 Piccadilly, London, W 1

First Published 1976
© 1976 Ronald Jasper, Peter Coughlan, David Jasper

Made and Printed in Great Britain
by Wm Collins Sons & Co Ltd Glasgow

Contents

Introduction

This little book could easily become your daily companion. On two facing pages, it offers prayers and readings for use each day, and it slips easily into a pocket or handbag. At work the book can easily be used at the lunch hour. At home it is the sort of thing you could pick up when you stop for a cup of tea or a coffee. Its purpose is to help us put a few moments aside, and so to become more aware of God's presence. Gradually, we begin to see the people we meet and the things we do in the light of his presence and his love.

The layout of the book

There are two main sections in the book. The first covers the seasons of the Christian year: seven days are offered for use during Advent, seven for Christmas, seven for Epiphanytide, seven for Lent, and seven for Eastertide. In this section of the book the readings and prayers express various aspects of each season. The second section offers four weeks for use during the rest of the year after Pentecost; and each day of the four weeks is built around a different theme.

In addition to these two major parts of the book, there is provision for special occasions, such as festivals of the Blessed Virgin Mary, the Apostles, Martyrs and so on. At the end of the book there are a number of blank pages, on which you can write any prayers of your own. These pages may be particularly useful if you wish to include schemes of intercessory prayers for regular daily or weekly use.

How to use the book

All you need for each day is given on two pages. In every case the day begins with an opening sentence. This indicates the theme chosen for the day or highlights an aspect of the season. The purpose of this brief sentence is to help you to pause for a moment and quietly renew your awareness of the presence of God. The mind and heart have to be still and quiet if we want to pray in spirit and in truth as our Lord Jesus Christ taught us.

The few verses of a psalm or poem or hymn that follow the sentence express the very heart of prayer and worship: to acknowledge who God is in praise and thanksgiving. The important thing here is not to rush through, but to take your

7

time. Haste is the death of prayer; so take it calmly and put other things aside.

The biblical reading and the reading which follows it form the bulk of what is given for each day. You will find that on some occasions one thought and on other occasions a different thought will strike you. After the readings pause for a while. Let the ideas lap around the mind. The readings may just lead you to be still in the presence of God, or they may lead you to pray.

Another point about the second reading is worth bearing in mind. We have deliberately chosen the passages from a wide variety of authors. It is our hope that people will be drawn to get hold of some of the books from which they have been taken. Many of them are in paperback, and some are of a kind that can often be bought at very little cost in a second-hand book shop. But we believe all are well worth reading.

The prayers which follow in the text for a given day are merely suggestions, launching-pads for your own prayer. If a group were to use the book, fuller prayers could be prepared beforehand or the various members of the group could be invited to pray spontaneously. The important thing is that the prayers should break out beyond our own needs and interests to the needs of others – those close to us and those far away.

The concluding prayers are mainly based on material that has been used for centuries in the public worship of Christians, and using them will almost certainly enrich our own prayer life.

When we pray the Lord's prayer at the end, we should be aware that we are joining in the prayer of Christians throughout the world. In fact we are sharing in the prayer of our Lord Jesus Christ before the Father; and it is the Holy Spirit who moves us to pray in sincerity of heart. The early Christians expressed it well when they prayed: Glory to the Father through the Son in the Spirit, now and for ever.

Individuals and groups

While the book will often be used by individuals, groups may also find it useful as a basis for their prayer together. The pattern of prayer, praise and reading given here has its kernel in the Daily Office books of the Christian Churches. This book is no substitute for those Offices, but it may well meet the need of many people who have never used them: and it may even encourage them to explore and use the Offices themselves.

Finally, we should like to thank those who assisted us in preparing this book, especially John Bell, Anthony Ingham, and Fergus Mulligan. This book was compiled by Christians of different denominations; it would be fitting if it were to be used by Christians, whatever their denomination. If Christians learn to pray together, the Churches will gradually grow into unity.

Advent: Sunday

Watch, for you do not know on what day your Lord is coming.

Matthew 24: 42

PSALM

Our God comes, he does not keep silence,
before him is a devouring fire,
around about him a mighty tempest.

He calls to the heavens above
and to the earth, that he may judge his people:

'Gather to me my faithful ones,
who make a covenant with me by sacrifice!'

The heavens declare his righteousness,
for God himself is judge!

Psalm 50 (49): 3–6

BIBLE READING

Jesus said: 'There will be signs in the sun and moon and stars; on earth nations in agony, bewildered by the clamour of the ocean and its waves; men dying of fear as they await what menaces the world, for the powers of heaven will be shaken. And then they will see the Son of Man coming in a cloud with power and great glory. When these things begin to take place, stand erect, hold your heads high, because your liberation is near at hand.

Watch yourselves, or your hearts will be coarsened with debauchery and drunkenness and the cares of life, and that day will be sprung on you suddenly, like a trap. For it will come down on every living man on the face of the earth. Stay awake, praying at all times for the strength to survive all that is going to happen, and to stand with confidence before the Son of Man.'

Luke 21: 25–8. 34–6

To prevent his disciples from questioning him about the time of his coming Christ said, 'Of that hour no one knows, neither the angels nor the Son. It is not for you to know the times or moments.' He hid the time from us so that we would be on the watch and so that each of us might think that the coming will happen in his own lifetime. If he had revealed when he was to come again, his coming would have been made pointless and the people and ages in which it will take place would no longer yearn for it. He said that he will come again but he did not say exactly when. Hence, all generations and ages live in eager expectation of him. The Lord's command about vigilance holds good for both parts of man. The body must avoid overpowering sleep and the soul must guard against sluggishness and timidity. In the words of scripture, 'Awake you just', and 'I rose up and am still with you', and 'Do not lose heart. That is why we do not lose heart in the ministry which is entrusted to us.'

St Ephraem, *Commentary on the Diatessaron*

PRAYERS

We pray that we may be
   ready to accept each day as it comes
   ready to respond to what the future may bring
We pray for
   those who provide us with news
   those who are frightened to face the future

Almighty God,
give us grace to cast away the works of darkness
and to put on the armour of light,
now in the time of this mortal life,
in which your Son Jesus Christ came to us in great humility:
so that on the last day,
when he shall come again in his glorious majesty
   to judge the living and the dead,
we may rise to the life immortal;
through him who is alive and reigns
   with you and the Holy Spirit,
one God, now and for ever.

Our Father

Watch, for you do not know on what day your Lord is coming.

11

Today, when you hear his voice, do not harden your hearts.

Hebrews 4: 7

PSALM

Render to the Lord the honour due to his name:
bring offerings and come into his courts.

O worship the Lord in the beauty of holiness:
let the whole earth dance in praise before him.

Let the fields rejoice, and everything in them:
then shall all the trees of the wood shout for joy before the Lord;

For he comes, he comes to judge the earth:
he shall judge the world with righteousness, and the peoples
with his truth.

Psalm 96 (95): 8–9. 12–13

BIBLE READING

It shall come to pass in the latter days
that the mountain of the house of the Lord
shall be established as the highest of the mountains,
and shall be raised above the hills;
and all the nations shall flow to it,
and many peoples shall come, and say:
'Come let us go up to the mountain of the Lord,
to the house of the God of Jacob;
that he may teach us his ways
and that we may walk in his paths.'
He shall judge between the nations,
and shall decide for many peoples;
and they shall beat their swords into ploughshares,
and their spears into pruning hooks;
nation shall not lift up sword against nation,
neither shall they learn war any more.

Isaiah 2: 2–4

Are we so deaf that we do not hear a loving God warning us that humanity is in danger of committing suicide? Are we so selfish that we do not hear the just God demanding that we do all we can to stop injustice suffocating the world and driving it to war? Are we so alienated that we can worship God at our ease in luxurious temples which are often empty in spite of all their liturgical pomp, and fail to see, hear and serve God where he is present and where he requires our presence, among mankind, the poor, the oppressed, the victims of injustice in which we ourselves are often involved? It is not difficult to hear God's call today in the world about us. It is difficult to do more than offer an emotional response, sorrow and regret. It is even more difficult to give up our comfort, break with old habits, let ourselves be moved by grace and change our life, be converted.

Dom Helder Camara, *The Desert is Fertile*

PRAYERS

We pray for
   true penitence and amendment of life
   the gift of peace to all men
   the work of the United Nations Organization and agencies
      working for peace
   the government of our country

Heavenly Father,
whose blessed Son was revealed
that he might destroy the works of the devil
and make us the sons of God
and heirs of eternal life:
grant that we, having this hope,
may purify ourselves even as he is pure;
that when he shall appear in power and great glory
we may be made like him in his eternal and glorious kingdom;
where he is alive and reigns with you and the Holy Spirit,
one God, now and for ever.

Our Father

Today, when you hear his voice, do not harden your hearts.

Advent: Tuesday

The holy scriptures are able to give you the wisdom that leads
to salvation through faith in Christ Jesus.

2 Timothy 2: 15

PSALM

Your word is a lamp for my steps
and a light for my path.

I have sworn and have determined
to obey your decrees.

Lord, I am deeply afflicted:
by your word give me life.

Accept, Lord, the homage of my lips
and teach me your decrees.

Your will is my heritage for ever,
the joy of my heart.

I set myself to carry out your statutes
in fullness, for ever.

Psalm 119 (118): 105–8. 111–12

BIBLE READING

Seek the Lord while he may be found,
call upon him while he is near.
For my thoughts are not your thoughts,
neither are your ways my ways, says the Lord.
For as the rain and the snow come down from heaven,
and return not thither but water the earth,
making it bring forth and sprout,
giving seed to the sower and bread to the eater,
so shall my word be that which goes forth from my mouth;
it shall not return to me empty,
but it shall accomplish that which I purpose
and prosper in the thing for which I sent it.

Isaiah 55: 6. 8. 10–11

The Old and New Testaments follow the same pattern in that they proceed from what has been wrought out in actual historical events to the implication of these events for the life of mankind. The meaning of Jehovah is revealed in the life, death and resurrection of Jesus Christ. And it is from the fact of Jesus Christ that the meaning of his Lordship becomes plain. Not only is there no 'other name under heaven, that is given among men, wherein we must be saved', but this salvation is something comparable with the act of creation itself . . . And Jesus Christ who has wrought this salvation is God's agent in creation . . . This unity of the creative and redemptive work of God in Jesus Christ who is the only Lord of men is the centre and focus of the Biblical teaching.

H. Cunliffe-Jones, *The Authority of the Biblical Revelation*

PRAYERS

We pray for
    those engaged in studying, translating and distributing the
      scriptures
    teachers of the Christian faith
    the Bible Reading Fellowship

Eternal God,
who caused all holy scriptures
    to be written for our learning:
help us so to hear them,
to read, mark, learn, and inwardly digest them
that, through patience, and the comfort of your holy Word,
we may embrace and for ever hold fast
    the hope of everlasting life,
which you have given us in our Saviour Jesus Christ.

Our Father

The holy scriptures are able to give you the wisdom that leads to salvation through faith in Christ Jesus.

15

Advent: Wednesday

Behold, your God will come and save you.

Isaiah 35: 4

PSALM

'O give thanks to the Lord for he is good;
for his great love is without end.'

Let them say this, the Lord's redeemed,
whom he redeemed from the land of the foe
and gathered from far-off lands,
from east and west, north and south.

Some wandered in the desert, in the wilderness,
finding no way to a city they could dwell in.

Then they cried to the Lord in their need
and he rescued them from their distress
and he led them along the right way,
to reach a city they could dwell in.

Psalm 107 (106): 1–4. 6–7

BIBLE READING

The wilderness and the dry land shall be glad,
the desert shall rejoice and blossom.
The glory of Lebanon shall be given to it,
the majesty of Carmel and Sharon.
They shall see the glory of the Lord,
the majesty of our God.

Strengthen the weak hands,
and make firm the feeble knees.
Say to those who are of a fearful heart,
'Be strong, fear not!
Behold, your God will come and save you'.

Then the eyes of the blind shall be opened,
and the ears of the deaf unstopped;
then shall the lame man leap like a hart,
and the tongue of the dumb sing for joy.
And the ransomed of the Lord shall return,
and come to him with singing,
with everlasting joy upon their heads.

Isaiah 35: 1–6. 10

We see a little group of adherents of Jesus, who had followed him from Galilee, overtaken at Jerusalem by the disaster of his death, yet within a very few days rising up and proclaiming the 'good news' that through this Jesus God is now to bring about what Josephus calls 'the revolution of the ages'. Plainly the reason is that Jesus had inspired in his followers something more than a Messianic *hope*. He was the source of an experience of which hope was but the efflorescence. He had proclaimed the advent of the world to come, but he had brought it as a moral and religious reality within the orbit of their spirit and in a way which henceforth linked their whole hope of God with him . . . It was not a case of an ardent Messianic hope leading men to believe in Jesus, but of an ardent faith in Jesus leading them to believe in the Messianic hope.

W. Manson, *Jesus the Messiah*

PRAYERS

We pray
   for the gift of hope for the future
   that men may put God before self
   that men may recognize God's hand at work
     in creation and redemption.

All-powerful God,
increase our strength of will for doing good
that Christ may find an eager welcome at his coming
and call us to his side in the kingdom of heaven
where he lives and reigns with you and the Holy Spirit,
one God, for ever and ever.

Our Father

Behold, your God will come and save you.

Advent: Thursday

Repent, for the kingdom of heaven is at hand.

Matthew 3: 2

POEM

There is a voice that cries:
Prepare a road for the Lord through the wilderness,
clear a highway across the desert for our God.

Every valley shall be lifted up,
every mountain and hill brought down;
rugged places shall be made smooth
and mountain-ranges become a plain.

Thus shall the glory of the Lord be revealed,
and all mankind together shall see it;
for the Lord himself has spoken.

Isaiah 40: 3–5

BIBLE READING

John appeared in the desert, baptizing people and preaching his message. 'Turn away from your sins and be baptized', he told the people, 'and God will forgive your sins.' Everybody from the region of Judea and the city of Jerusalem went out to hear John. They confessed their sins and he baptized them in the Jordan river.

John wore clothes made of camel's hair, with a leather belt round his waist; he ate locusts and wild honey. He announced to the people, 'The man who will come after me is much greater than I am; I am not good enough even to bend down and untie his sandals. I baptize you with water, but he will baptize you with the Holy Spirit.'

Mark 1: 4–8

The impact that John the Baptist made did not depend on trite exhortations to be good. This formidable ascetic, haunting the wilderness in his uncouth garments, revived the popular image of an inspired prophet, and like the ancient prophets he announced the impending judgment of God on a recreant people. The 'Coming One', he said, would soon be here, a terrifying figure, like a woodman laying about him with his axe, like a winnower separating grain from chaff. Indeed (and it was this that gave John's preaching its bite) he was here already, unknown, biding his time ... His (John's) task was, says Luke, 'to prepare a people that shall be fit for the Lord'. That was what he was doing when he urged moral reformation and baptized those who were ready to commit themselves to it ... But baptism in water, he insisted, was only preparatory. The Coming One would 'baptize with spirit and fire' – a strongly emotive phrase which we need not try to spell out. Meanwhile, they were to mend their ways and wait – but not for long.

C. H. Dodd, *The Founder of Christianity*

PRAYERS

We pray for
the inmates of prisons, approved schools and detention centres
those who are at odds with society
all social workers and staffs of remedial institutions
those who are indifferent to the Gospel

Almighty God,
who sent out your servant John the Baptist
to prepare your people for the coming of your Son:
inspire the ministers and stewards of your truth
to turn our disobedient hearts to the law of love;
that when he comes again in glory,
we may stand with confidence before him as our judge;
who is alive and reigns with you and the Holy Spirit,
one God, now and for ever.

Our Father

Repent, for the kingdom of heaven is at hand.

Advent: Friday

Behold, I am the handmaid of the Lord; let it be to me according to your word.

Luke 1: 38

POEM *'Thanks and a plea to Mary'*

I thank you, gentle lady,
with gracious heart so mild,
For that good you have done me
With your sweet child.

You are good and sweet and bright,
chosen from all others.
The blessed child your heart's delight,
My Lord Jesus.

Gentle maid, to you I pray
And to your blessed baby,
For shelter, wherein I might stay
And find God's mercy.

Mary, mother, look on me,
with your loving eyes,
Granting rest and bliss to me,
Lady, when I die.

A Medieval English Lyric

BIBLE READING

In the sixth month the angel Gabriel was sent from God to a city of Galilee named Nazareth, to a virgin betrothed to a man whose name was Joseph, of the house of David; and the virgin's name was Mary. And he came to her and said, 'O favoured one, the Lord is with you!' But she was greatly troubled at the saying and considered in her mind what sort of greeting this might be. And the angel said to her, 'Do not be afraid, Mary, for you have found favour with God. And behold you will conceive in your womb and bear a son, and you shall call his name Jesus.'

And Mary said, 'Behold, I am the handmaid of the Lord; let it be to me according to your word.' And the angel departed from her.

Luke 1: 26–33. 38

Jesus Christ first came into the world because of Mary's free and loving 'yes'. He continues to come into the world, however, because of our free and loving 'yes' . . . Every day, we must choose our lives anew – that is, the people who are around us, the places where we are, the things in which we participate. All of that life must become ours; for that life is the 'daily bread' that we must assimilate into ourselves. At the same time, we must offer it to Christ, who asks for it. We must allow Christ to transform it within himself and assimilate it totally so that – with our help – he may actualize the mystery of his Incarnation. For man's free and loving 'yes' to his present life is the key to the mystical Incarnation of Jesus which lies at the heart of creation.

Michel Quoist, *Christ is Alive*

PRAYERS

We pray for
   the joyful acceptance of all that life brings
   the sick and the suffering
   the handicapped and the lonely
   those waiting for the birth of their children

Heavenly Father,
who chose the Virgin Mary, full of grace,
to be the mother of our Lord and Saviour:
fill us with your grace,
that in all things we may accept your holy will
and with her rejoice in your salvation;
through Jesus Christ our Lord.

Our Father

Behold, I am the handmaid of the Lord; let it be to me according to your word.

Advent: Saturday

He will be called Emmanuel, which means, 'God is with us'

Matthew 1: 23.

POEM *The Call*

Come, my Way, my Truth, my Life:
Such a Way, as gives us breath:
Such a Truth, as ends all strife:
Such a Life, as killeth death.

Come, my Light, my Feast, my Strength:
Such a Light, as shows a feast:
Such a Feast, as mends in strength:
Such a Strength, as makes his guest.

Come, my Joy, my Love, my Heart:
Such a Joy, as none can move:
Such a Love, as none can part:
Such a Heart, as joyes in Love.

George Herbert

BIBLE READING

This was the way that Jesus Christ was born. His mother Mary was engaged to Joseph, but before they were married she found out that she was going to have a baby by the Holy Spirit. Joseph, to whom she was engaged, was a man who always did what was right; but he did not want to disgrace Mary publicly, so he made plans to break the engagement secretly. While he was thinking about this, an angel of the Lord appeared to him in a dream and said, 'Joseph, descendant of David, do not be afraid to take Mary to be your wife. For it is by the Holy Spirit that she has conceived. She will give birth to a son and you will name him Jesus, because he will save his people from their sins'. Now all this happened in order to make come true what the Lord had said through the prophet, 'The virgin will become pregnant and give birth to a son, and he will be called Emmanuel' which means, 'God is with us.'

Matthew 1:18–23

In the Church Militant, by daily contact with the Messiah by the means of His Word, His Sacraments, and the members of His mystical Body, human nature is purged and is transformed, becoming conformed to the image of the Son. Here is the means, provided by God, whereby the renewal of heart and spirit which Jeremiah and Ezekiel foretold can at last take place. They saw that it must be; they did not know how. They could not see beforehand, as we can see after it has happened, that it could only be through a Divine Intervention, through God coming in person to fight His own battle, and taking on Him the form of the Servant.

G. Hebert, *The Throne of David*

PRAYERS

We pray for
  the unity of the Church
  the life and witness of the Church
  the leaders of our own church
  members of our own congregation

God of power and mercy
open our hearts in welcome.
Remove the things that hinder us
  from receiving Christ with joy,
so that we may share his wisdom
and become one with him
when he comes in glory,
for he lives and reigns with you and the Holy Spirit,
one God, for ever and ever.

Our Father

He will be called Emmanuel, which means, 'God is with us.'

Christmas: Sunday

To you is born this day a Saviour, who is Christ the Lord.

Luke 2: 11

PSALM

I will hear what the Lord God has to say,
a voice that speaks of peace,
peace for his people and his friends
and those who turn to him in their hearts.
His help is near for those who fear him
and his glory will dwell in our land.

Mercy and faithfulness have met;
justice and peace have embraced.
Faithfulness shall spring from the earth
and justice look down from heaven.

Psalm 85 (84): 9–12

BIBLE READING

While they were in Bethlehem, the time came for Mary to be delivered. And she gave birth to her first-born son and wrapped him in swaddling cloths, and laid him in a manger, because there was no place for them in the inn. And in that region there were shepherds out in the field, keeping watch over their flock by night. And an angel of the Lord appeared to them, and the glory of the Lord shone around them, and they were filled with fear. And the angel said to them, 'Be not afraid; for behold, I will bring you good news of a great joy which will come to all the people; for to you is born this day in the city of David a Saviour, who is Christ the Lord. And this will be a sign for you; you will find a babe wrapped in swaddling cloths and lying in a manger.' And suddenly there was with the angel a multitude of the heavenly host praising God and saying, 'Glory to God in the highest, and on earth peace among men with whom he is pleased!'

Luke 2: 6–14

SECOND READING

Mary holds her finger out, and a divine hand closes on it. The maker of the world is born a begging child; he begs for milk, and does not know that it is milk for which he begs. We will not lift our hands to pull the love of God down to us, but he lifts his hands to pull human compassion down upon his cradle. So the weakness of God proves stronger than men, and the folly of God proves wiser than men. Love is the strongest instrument of omnipotence, for accomplishing those tasks he cares most dearly to perform; and this is how he brings his love to bear on human pride; by weakness not by strength, by need and not by bounty.

A. Farrer, *Said or Sung*

PRAYERS

We pray for
  families and home life
  those who are absent from home
  those who find home life difficult
  children
  children's homes

Eternal God,
who made this most holy night
to shine with the brightness of your one true light:
bring us to have known the revelation of that light on earth,
to see the radiance of your heavenly glory;
through Jesus Christ our Lord.

Our Father

To you is born this day a Saviour, who is Christ the Lord.

Christmas: Monday

The Word was made flesh, he lived among us, and we saw his glory.

John 1: 14

HYMN *Te Deum*

You, Christ, are the King of glory,
the eternal Son of the Father.
When you became man to set us free
you did not abhor the Virgin's womb.
You overcame the sting of death,
and opened the kingdom of heaven to all believers.
You are seated at God's right hand in glory.
We believe that you will come, and be our judge.
    Come then, Lord, and help your people,
    bought with the price of your own blood,
    and bring us with your saints
    to glory everlasting.

BIBLE READING

In the beginning was the Word: and the Word was with God and the Word was God. He was with God in the beginning. Through him all things came to be, not one thing had its being but through him. All that came to be had life in him and that life was the light of men, a light that shines in the dark, a light that darkness could not overpower.

The Word was the true light that enlightens all men; and he was coming into the world. The Word was made flesh, he lived among us, and we saw his glory, the glory that is his as the only Son of the Father, full of grace and truth.

John 1: 1–5. 9–14

Revelation shows that the merely unitarian God found in post-Christian Judaism, in Islam, and throughout the modern consciousness does not exist. At the heart of that mystery which the Church expresses in her teaching of the trinity of persons in the unity of life stands the God of Revelation. Here John seeks the root of Christ's existence: in the second of the Most Holy Persons; the Word, in whom God the Speaker reveals the fullness of his being. The Second 'Countenance' of God, here called Word, is also named Son, since he who speaks the Word is known as Father.

Son of God become man – not only descended to inhabit a human frame, but 'become' man – literally; and in order that no possible doubt arise (that, for example, it may never be asserted that Christ, despising the lowliness of the body, had united himself only with the essence of a holy soul or with an exalted spirit), John specifies sharply: Christ 'was made flesh'. He presents it austerely . . . Nothing here of the wealth of lovely characterization and intimate detail that makes Luke's account bloom so richly. Everything is concentrated on the ultimate, all-powerful essentials: Word, flesh, step into the world; the eternal origin, the tangible earthly reality, the mystery of unity.

Romano Guardini, *The Lord*

PRAYERS

We pray for
  the Church
  young churches
  our local church
  the ordained ministries of the Church.

Lord God,
we praise you for creating man,
and still more for restoring him in Christ.
Your Son shared our weakness:
may we share his glory,
for he lives and reigns with you and the Holy Spirit,
one God, for ever and ever.

Our Father

The Word was made flesh, he lived among us, and we saw his glory.

Christmas: Tuesday

He emptied himself, taking the form of a servant.

Philippians 2: 7

PSALM

O sing to the Lord a new song:
for he has done marvellous things.

The Lord has made known his salvation:
he has revealed his righteousness in the sight of the nations.

He has remembered his mercy and faithfulness towards the
   house of Israel:
and all the ends of the earth have seen the salvation of our God.

Shout with joy to the Lord, all the earth:
break into singing and make melody.

Make melody to the Lord upon the harp:
upon the harp and with the voice of praise.

With trumpets and with horns:
cry out in triumph before the Lord, the King.

Psalm 98 (97): 1. 3–7

BIBLE READING

Though he was in the form of God, Jesus did not count equality
with God a thing to be grasped, but emptied himself, taking the
form of a servant, being born in the likeness of men. And being
found in human form he humbled himself and became obedient
unto death, even death on a cross. Therefore God has highly
exalted him and bestowed on him the name which is above every
name, that at the name of Jesus every knee should bow, in
heaven and on earth and under the earth, and every tongue
confess that Jesus Christ is Lord, to the glory of God the Father.

Philippians 2: 6–11

For a Christian there is nothing particularly difficult about Christmas in a prison cell. I daresay it will have more meaning and will be observed with greater sincerity here in this prison than in places where all that survives of the feast is its name. That misery, suffering, poverty, loneliness, helplessness and guilt look different to the eyes of God from what they do to man, that God should come down to the very place which men usually abhor, that Christ was born in a stable because there was no room for him in the inn – these are things which a prisoner can understand better than anyone else. For him the Christmas story is glad tidings in a very real sense. And that faith gives him a part in the communion of saints, a fellowship transcending the bounds of time and space and reducing the months of confinement here to insignificance.

On Christmas Eve I shall be thinking of you all very much, and I want you to believe that I too shall have a few hours of real joy, and that I am not allowing my troubles to get the better of me.

D. Bonhoeffer, *Letters and Papers from Prison*

PRAYERS

We pray for
   the homeless, the lonely, the forsaken
   those who seek to alleviate misery and distress
   the social services

Almighty God,
who wonderfully created us in your own image
and yet more wonderfully restored us
through your Son Jesus Christ:
grant that, as he came to share in our humanity,
so we may share the life of his divinity;
who is alive and reigns with you and the Holy Spirit,
one God, now and for ever.

Our Father

     He emptied himself, taking the form of a servant.

Christmas: Wednesday

Glory to God in the highest.

Luke 2: 14

I will sing for ever of your love, O Lord,
through all the ages my mouth will proclaim your truth.
Of this I am sure, that your love lasts for ever,
that your truth is firmly established as the heavens.

I have made a covenant with my chosen one;
I have sworn to David my servant:
I will establish your dynasty for ever
and set up your throne through all ages.

The heavens proclaim your wonders, O Lord;
the assembly of your holy ones proclaims your truth.
For who in the skies can compare with the Lord
Or who is like the Lord among the sons of God?

Psalm 80 (88): 2–7

BIBLE READING

He is the image of the invisible God, the firstborn of all creation;
for in him all things were created, in heaven and on earth, visible
and invisible, whether thrones or dominions or principalities or
authorities – all things were created through him and for him.
He is before all things, and in him all things hold together. He is
the head of the body, the Church; he is the beginning, the first-
born from the dead, that in everything he might be pre-eminent.
For in him all the fullness of God was pleased to dwell, and
through him to reconcile to himself all things, whether on earth
or in heaven, making peace by the blood of his cross.

Colossians 1. 15–20

The prodigious expanses of time which preceded the first Christmas were not empty of Christ: they were imbued with the influx of his power. It was the ferment of his conception that stirred up the cosmic masses and directed the initial developments of the biosphere. It was the travail preceding his birth that accelerated the development of instinct and the birth of thought upon the earth. Let us have done with the stupidity which makes a stumbling-block of the endless eras of expectancy imposed on us by the Messiah; the fearful, anonymous labours of primitive man, the beauty fashioned through its age-long history by ancient Egypt, the anxious expectancies of Israel, the patient distilling of the attar of oriental mysticism, the endless refining of wisdom by the Greeks: all these were needed before the Flower could blossom on the rod of Jesse and of all humanity. All these preparatory processes were cosmically and biologically necessary that Christ might set foot upon our human stage. And all this labour was set in motion by the active, creative awakening of his soul inasmuch as that human soul had been chosen to breathe life into the universe. When Christ first appeared before men in the arms of Mary he had already stirred up the world.

T. de Chardin, *Hymn of the Universe*

PRAYERS

We pray for
    those engaged in creative work, both mental and physical
    schools, colleges and universities
    work training schemes
    the unemployed

All praise to you, Almighty God and heavenly King,
who sent your Son into the world
to take our nature upon him
and to be born of a pure virgin:
grant that, as we are born again in him,
so he may continually dwell in us
and reign on earth as he reigns in heaven
with you and the Holy Spirit
now and for ever.

Our Father

        Glory to God in the highest.

Christmas: Thursday

God has bestowed on him the name which is above every name.

Philippians 2: 9

HYMN *I sing of a maiden*

I sing of a maiden
That is matchless:
King of all kings
For her son she chose.

He came all so still
Where his mother was,
As dew in April
That falls on the grass.

He came all so still
Where his mother lay,
As dew in April
That falls on the spray.

Mother and maiden
Was none but she;
Well may such a lady
God's mother be.

BIBLE READING

The shepherds went with haste, and found Mary and Joseph, and the babe lying in a manger. And when they saw it they made known the saying which had been told them concerning this child; and all who had heard it wondered at what the shepherds told them. But Mary kept all these things, pondering them in her heart. And the shepherds returned, glorifying and praising God for all that they had heard and seen, as it had been told them. And at the end of eight days, when he was circumcised, he was called Jesus, the name given by the angel before he was conceived in the womb.

Luke 2: 16–21

The word Messiah means the anointed one: the Greek word is Christos . . . This word has long since been turned into a proper name, a part of the name Jesus Christ. Originally, however, 'Messiah' was a title, borne by the ancient Kings of Israel. The King was accounted the one anointed by God *per se*, and even during the period of the kings of Judah the hope of a future king grew up, a king who would perfect the king's function of ruling in the name of God over Israel and the world in peace and righteousness. Although Jesus rejected the title of Christ for himself, it was later assigned to him . . . The bringer of salvation whom the Jewish people expected in the figure of the Messiah was, after all, actually Jesus, even if in a different form from what the Messianic hopes had imagined.

W. Pannenberg, *The Apostles' Creed*

PRAYERS

We pray for
   rulers and governments
   those who hold responsible positions in the state
   civic and local authorities
   the Civil Service

Lord God,
we praise you for creating man,
and still more for restoring him in Christ.
Your Son shared our weakness:
may we share his glory,
for he lives and reigns with you and the Holy Spirit,
one God, for ever and ever.

Our Father

God has bestowed on him that name which is above every name.

Christmas: Friday

There is a child born for us, a son given to us.

Isaiah 9: 5–6

PSALM

O Lord, you once favoured your land
and revived the fortunes of Jacob,
your forgave the guilt of your people
and covered all their sins.

I will hear what the Lord God has to say,
a voice that speaks of peace,
peace for his people and his friends
and those who turn to him in their hearts.
His help is near for those who fear him
and his glory will dwell in our land.

The Lord will make us prosper
and our earth shall yield its fruit.
Justice shall march before him
and peace shall follow his steps.

Psalm 85 (84): 2–3. 9–10. 13–14

BIBLE READING

There is a child born for us,
a son given to us
and dominion is laid on his shoulders;
and this is the name they give him:
Wonder-Counsellor, Mighty-God,
Eternal-Father, Prince-of-Peace.
Wide is his dominion
in a peace that has no end,
for the throne of David
and for his royal power,
which he establishes and makes secure
in justice and integrity.
From this time onwards and for ever,
the jealous love of the Lord of hosts will do this.

Isaiah 9: 5-7

When God became incarnate as man his meaningfulness as God came into its own. The self-giving, the becoming-man, the suffering love were not additions to the divine experience or mere incidents in the divine history. In becoming man, God revealed the meaning of what it is to be God. But he could do so not because he is incomplete without man or dependent upon creatures for his own existence, but because he is in himself the perfection of love. The glory is seen in the becoming-man because it is a glory 'beyond' and eternal. So, too, in Jesus the human race finds its own true meaning . . . Man's true glory is the reflection in him of the divine glory, the self-giving love seen in Jesus.

A. M. Ramsey, *God, Christ and the World*

PRAYERS

We pray for
  charitable organizations
  those involved in youth work
  missionary societies

Almighty God,
your Son has opened for us
a new and living way into your presence.
Give us pure hearts and steadfast wills
to worship you in spirit and in truth;
through the same Jesus Christ our Lord.

Our Father

There is a child born for us, a son given to us.

Christmas: Saturday

Let us love one another, since love comes from God.

1 John 4: 7

HYMN *Love Unknown*

My song is love unknown,
My Saviour's love to me,
Love to the loveless shown,
That they might lovely be.
O who am I,
That for my sake
My Lord should take
Frail flesh, and die?

He came from his blest throne,
Salvation to bestow;
But men made strange, and none
The longed-for Christ would know.
But O, my friend,
My friend indeed,
Who at my need
His life did spend!

Samuel Crossman

BIBLE READING

Whatever we ask God we shall receive, because we keep his commandments and live the kind of life that he wants. His commandments are these: that we believe in the name of his Son Jesus Christ and that we love one another as he told us to.

My dear people, let us love one another since love comes from God and everyone who loves is begotten by God and knows God. Anyone who fails to love can never have known God because God is love. God's love for us was revealed when God sent into the world his only Son so that we could have life through him; this is the love I mean: not our love for God, but God's love for us when he sent his Son to be the sacrifice that takes our sins away.

1 John 3: 22-3. 4. 7–10

Love, of course, means something much more than mere sentiment, much more than token favours and perfunctory almsdeeds.
Love means an interior and spiritual identification with one's
brother, so that he is not regarded as an 'object' to 'which' one
'does good'. The fact is that good done to another is of little or
no spiritual value. Love takes one's neighbour as one's other self,
and loves him with all the immense humility and discretion and
reserve and reverence without which no one can presume to enter
into the sanctuary of another's subjectivity . . .

The charity of the Desert Fathers is not set before us in
unconvincing effusions. The full difficulty and magnitude of the
task of loving others is recognized everywhere and never min-
imized. It is hard to really love others if love is taken in the full
sense of the word. Love demands a complete inner transformation . . . we have to become in a sense, the person we love. And
this involves a kind of death of our own being, our own self.

Thomas Merton, *The Call of the Desert*

PRAYERS

We pray for
    the peace of the world
    the United Nations Organization
    the Red Cross, Christian Aid, and international relief agencies.

Almighty God,
you have taught us through your Son
that love is the fulfilling of the law.
Grant that we may love you with our whole heart
and our neighbours as ourselves;
through Jesus Christ our Lord.

Our Father

Let us love one another, since love comes from God.

Epiphany: Sunday

Nations shall come to your light, and Kings to the brightness of your rising.

Isaiah 60: 3

PSALM

O God give your judgment to the king,
to a king's son your justice,
that he may judge your people in justice
and your poor in right judgment.

He shall endure like the sun and the moon
from age to age.
He shall descend like rain on the meadow,
like raindrops on the earth.

Before him his enemies shall fall,
his foes lick the dust.
The kings of Tharsis and the sea coasts
shall pay him tribute.

The kings of Sheba and Seba
shall bring him gifts.
Before him all kings shall fall prostrate,
all nations shall serve him.

Psalm 72 (71): 1–2. 5–6. 9–11

BIBLE READING

Herod summoned the wise men secretly and ascertained from them what time the star appeared; and he sent them to Bethlehem saying, 'Go and search diligently for the child, and when you have found him bring me word, that I too may come and worship him.' When they had heard the king they went their way; and lo, the star which they had seen in the East went before them, till it came to rest over the place where the child was. When they saw the star, they rejoiced exceedingly with great joy; and going into the house they saw the child with Mary his mother, and they fell down and worshipped him. Then, opening their treasures, they offered him gifts, gold and frankincense and myrrh.

Matthew 2: 7–11

There is a light which is for ever in motion, and can be retained only by moving with it. There is a light which is always just ahead of where you stand. You must follow it if you would arrive: and the following must never cease. Those Wise Men from the hidden East did but 'follow the gleam' which broke in upon their patient studies. And all the Epiphanies of the Lord do but tell of the gleams that come and go, and that mean so much as they pass. The Epiphanies should be alive among us. And everywhere men should be rising to follow the gleam. Here is a wearying, suffering, starving world close round you. What are you doing to help it? There are promptings to be obeyed. There are ventures that might be made. Why not? have you not caught sight of His star? Oh! Rise and follow!

From a sermon by Henry Scott Holland, in A. C. Bouquet,
A Lectionary of Christian Prose

PRAYERS

We pray for
   kings and rulers
   those who bear responsibility of government
   those who serve in local government
   civil servants

Eternal God,
who by the shining of a star
led the wise men to the worship of your Son:
guide by your light the nations of the earth,
that the whole world may behold your glory;
through Jesus Christ our Lord.

Our Father

Nations shall come to your light, and kings to the brightness of your rising.

Epiphany: Monday

Those who are led by God's Spirit are God's sons.

Romans 8: 14

Lord, how I love your law!
It is ever in my mind.
Your command makes me wiser than my foes;
for it is mine for ever.
I have more insight than all who teach me
for I ponder your will.
I have more understanding than the old
for I keep your precepts.
I turn my feet from evil paths
to obey your word.
I have not turned away from your decrees;
you yourself have taught me.

Psalm 119 (118): 97–102

BIBLE READING

Every year the parents of Jesus went to Jerusalem for the Feast
of the Passover. When Jesus was twelve years old, they went to
the feast as usual. When the days of the feast were over they
started back home, but the boy Jesus stayed in Jerusalem. His
parents did not know this. On the third day they found him in
the temple, sitting with the Jewish teachers, listening to them and
asking questions. All who heard him were amazed at his intelli-
gent answers. His mother said to him, 'Son, why have you done
this to us. Your father and I have been terribly worried trying to
find you.' He answered them, 'Why did you have to look for me?
Didn't you know that I had to be in my Father's house?'

Luke 2: 41–3. 46–9

The boyish incident – recorded by St Luke – of His remaining behind in Jerusalem after His first Passover feast, when His parents and the rest of their company had set out on their homeward journey, is an illuminating one . . . His listening and questioning with the doctors in the Temple – the expert exponents of the Scriptures – showed how he valued all the living spiritual deposit contained in recorded Jewish history and prophecy . . . 'Ask – seek – knock: for every one that asketh receiveth; and he that seeketh findeth; and to him that knocketh it shall be opened': in maturity He was to counsel this His childhood's active questioning way as *the* spiritual way for all to truth, and life and fulfilment. His 'Verily I say unto you, Except ye turn, and become as little children, ye shall in no wise enter the Kingdom of Heaven', was spoken out of His own experience in entering as a child into this Kingdom.

Maisie Spens, *Concerning Himself*

PRAYERS

We pray for
   children
   parents
   those responsible for teaching the young
   children's homes

Give us, Lord, we pray,
the Spirit to think and to do always
   those things that are right:
that we who can do no good thing without you
may have power to live
   according to your holy will;
through Jesus Christ our Lord.

Our Father

   Those who are led by God's Spirit are God's sons.

Epiphany: Tuesday

You are my Son, the Beloved; my favour rests on you.

Mark 1: 11

PSALM

O give the Lord you sons of God
give the Lord glory and power;
Give the Lord the glory of his name.
Adore the Lord in his holy court.

The Lord's voice resounding on the waters,
the Lord on the immensity of waters;
the voice of the Lord, full of power,
the voice of the Lord, full of splendour.
The Lord will give strength to his people,
the Lord will bless his people with peace.

Psalm 29 (28): 1–4. 11

BIBLE READING

Jesus went from Galilee to the Jordan and came to John to be
baptized by him. But John tried to make him change his mind.
'I ought to be baptized by you,' John said, 'yet you come to me!'
But Jesus answered him, 'Let it be so for now. For in this way
we shall do all that God requires.' So John agreed. As soon as
he was baptized, Jesus came up out of the water. Then heaven
was opened to him, and he saw the Spirit of God coming down
like a dove and lighting on him. And then a voice said from
heaven, 'This is my own dear Son, with whom I am well pleased.'

Matthew 3: 13–17

Though Jesus was baptized with others, it was recognized that no other baptism was strictly comparable to His, for He was baptized as the Messiah. Therein He commenced His messianic ministry with a view to the bringing in of the new creation; therein He was acknowledged by the Father as the Christ; therein the Spirit came to Him, to manifest through Him the Kingdom in grace and power . . . Because our Lord's baptism was messianic, it could not be unrelated to our baptism. As in all His messianic action, Jesus makes His baptism a medium for His mediatorial and creative activity, but the identical outward action in our case expresses our dependence on Him and receptivity of the fruits of His action.

G. R. Beasley-Murray, *Baptism in the New Testament*

PRAYERS

We pray for
   the missionary work of the Church
   missionary societies
   those who are preparing for baptism
   those who have not heard the Gospel

Almighty, ever-living God,
when Christ was baptized in the river Jordan
the Holy Spirit came upon him
and your voice proclaimed from heaven
   'This is my beloved Son'.
Grant that we,
who by water and the Holy Spirit are your adopted children,
may continue steadfast in your love.
We make our prayer through our Lord Jesus Christ your Son,
who lives and reigns with you and the Holy Spirit,
God, for ever and ever.

Our Father

   You are my Son, the Beloved, my favour rests on you.

Epiphany: Wednesday

This is a true saying, to be completely accepted and believed:
Christ Jesus came into the world to save sinners.

1 Timothy 1.15

PSALM

I waited patiently for the Lord;
he inclined to me and heard my cry.
He drew me up from the desolate pit,
out of the miry bog,
and set my feet upon a rock,
making my steps secure.
He put a new song in my mouth,
a song of praise to our God.
Many will see and fear,
and put their trust in the Lord.

Psalm 40 (39): 1–3

BIBLE READING

As Jesus walked along he saw a tax collector, Levi, the son of
Alphaeus, sitting in his office. Jesus said to him, 'Follow me'.
Levi got up and followed him. Later on Jesus was having a meal
in Levi's home. A large number of tax collectors and outcasts
was following Jesus, and many of them joined him and his
disciples, at table. Some leaders of the Law, who were Pharisees,
saw that Jesus was eating with these outcasts and tax collectors;
so they asked his disciples, 'Why does he eat with such people?'
Jesus heard them and answered, 'People who are well do not
need a doctor, but only those who are sick. I have not come to
call the respectable people, but the outcasts.'

Mark 2: 14–17

Well, about a year and a half afterwards, that wicked sinful thought of which I have spoken before, went through my wicked heart, even this thought, 'Let Christ go if he will . . . '. I never saw such heights and depths in grace and love, and mercy, as I saw after this temptation. Great sins do draw out great grace; and where guilt is most terrible and fierce there the mercy of God in Christ, when showed to the soul, appears most high and mighty . . . Many other things I might here make observation of, but I would be brief, and therefore shall at this time omit them, and do pray God that my harms may make others fear to offend, lest they also be made to bear the iron yoke that I did. I had two or three times, at or about my deliverance from this temptation, such strange apprehensions of the grace of God, that I could hardly bear up under it, it was so out of measure amazing.

John Bunyan, *Grace Abounding to the Chief of Sinners*

PRAYERS

We pray for
  the victims of sin
  the outcasts of society
  staffs of prisons and remand homes
  welfare workers and those engaged in rescue work

Merciful Lord,
grant to your faithful people
  pardon and peace:
that we may be cleansed from all our sins
and serve you with a quiet mind;
through Jesus Christ our Lord.

Our Father

This is a true saying, to be completely accepted and believed:
Christ Jesus came into the world to save sinners.

Epiphany: Thursday

Heaven and earth will pass away; my words will never pass away.

Mark 12: 31

PSALM

The law of the Lord is perfect and revives the soul.
The Lord's instruction never fails,
and makes the simple wise.
The precepts of the Lord are right and rejoice the heart.
The commandment of the Lord shines clear
and gives light to the eyes.
The fear of the Lord is pure and abides for ever.
The Lord's decrees are true and righteous every one,
more to be desired than gold, pure gold in plenty,
sweeter than syrup or honey from the comb.

Psalm 19 (18): 7–10

BIBLE READING

Some Pharisees and some members of Herod's party were sent
to Jesus to trap him with questions. They came to him and said,
'Father, we know that you tell the truth, without worrying about
what people think. You pay no attention to a man's status, but
teach the truth about God's will for man. Tell us, is it against our
Law to pay taxes to the Roman Emperor? Should we pay them,
or not?' But Jesus saw through their trick and answered, 'Why
are you trying to trap me? Bring a silver coin, and let me see it.'
They brought him one and he asked, 'Whose face and name are
these?' 'The Emperor's', they answered. So Jesus said, 'Well,
then, pay to the Emperor what belongs to him, and pay to God
what belongs to God.' And they were filled with wonder at him.

Mark 12: 13–17

When you and I venture to listen to another person 'in the name of Jesus Christ' there is an unseen listener present, Jesus himself. We have to listen to him listening. We have to know Jesus and be ready to learn all his meanings too. And in the context of this listening it may be that he will have something new to say, something we have never heard before. And if we listen very carefully, with concentrated attention, it is likely that we will hear him speaking to us through the lips of a Hindu, a Muslim, a Buddhist, a Jew, a man or woman of some tribal religion – or nearer home, a Marxist, or a humanist. Jesus, now as always, is very full of surprises.

M. A. C. Warren, 'A Theology of Attention', in
Face to Face: Essays on Inter-faith Dialogue

PRAYERS

We pray for
  teachers and scholars
  universities, colleges and schools
  those engaged in work of communication
  those who work on radio and television

Eternal God,
whose Son Jesus Christ is for all mankind
  the way, the truth, and the life:
grant us to walk in his way,
to rejoice in his truth,
and to share his risen life;
who is alive and reigns with you and the Holy Spirit,
one God, now and for ever.

Our Father

Heaven and earth will pass away; my words will never pass away.

Epiphany: Friday

We have heard the Word of life, and we have seen it with our eyes.

1 John 1: 1

PSALM

Let God be gracious to us and bless us:
and make his face shine upon us;

That your ways may be known on earth:
your liberating power among all nations.

Let the peoples praise you, O God:
let all the peoples praise you.

Let the nations be glad and sing:
for you judge the peoples with integrity, and govern the nations
upon earth.

Psalm 67 (66): 1–4

BIBLE READING

There was a wedding at Cana in Galilee. The mother of Jesus
was there, and Jesus and his disciples had also been invited.
When they ran out of wine, since the wine provided for the
wedding was all finished, the mother of Jesus said to him, 'They
have no wine.' Jesus said, 'Woman, why turn to me? My hour
has not yet come.' His mother said to the servants, 'Do whatever
he tells you'. There were six stone water jars standing there,
meant for the ablutions that are customary among the Jews: each
could hold twenty or thirty gallons. Jesus said to the servants,
'Fill the jars with water', and they filled them to the brim. 'Draw
some out now', he told them, 'and take it to the steward'. They
did this; the steward tasted the water, and it had turned into
wine.

John 2: 1–9

The wedding feast lacked wine, not water, yet it is precisely to the water, concerned with the admission to the feast by purification, that Jesus turns to supply the deficiency of wine. And this is the significant part of the miracle. That which had, as water, never been able, and never would be able, in any quantity, large or small, to prepare men by an adequate purification to enter worthily into an earthly marriage or union of persons, was to turn, in the presence of the true bridegroom, and by his grace and power, into the very substance of the joy of the divine marriage between God and his people. The inadequate and insufficient preparatory water became the more than adequate and superabundant wine of actual celebration and enjoyment.

J. Marsh, *Saint John*

PRAYERS

We pray for
  the Church
  Church societies and organizations
  religious communities

Almighty God,
in Christ you make all things new.
Transform the poverty of our nature
  by the riches of your grace,
and in the renewal of our lives
make known your heavenly glory;
through Jesus Christ our Lord.

Our Father

We have heard the Word of Life, and we have seen it with our eyes.

Epiphany: Saturday

Come to me, all of you who are tired from carrying your heavy loads, and I will give you rest.

Matthew 11: 28

HYMN *How sweet the name of Jesus*

How sweet the name of Jesus sounds
In a believer's ear!
It soothes his sorrows, heals his wounds,
And drives away his fear.

It makes the wounded spirit whole,
And calms the troubled breast;
'Tis manna to the hungry soul,
And to the weary rest.

Dear name! The rock on which I build,
My shield and hiding-place,
My never-failing treasury filled
With boundless stores of grace.

J. Newton

BIBLE READING

They came to Jericho. As Jesus was leaving with his disciples and a large crowd, a blind man named Bartimaeus, the son of Timaeus, was sitting by the road, begging. When he heard that it was Jesus of Nazareth, he began to shout 'Jesus! Son of David! Have mercy on me!' Many scolded him and told him to be quiet. But he shouted even more loudly, 'Son of David, have mercy on me!' Jesus stopped and said, 'Call him.' So they called the blind man. 'Cheer up!' they said. 'Get up, he is calling you'. He threw off his cloak, jumped up and came to Jesus. 'What do you want me to do for you?' Jesus asked him. 'Teacher', the blind man answered, 'I want to see again'. 'Go', Jesus told him, 'your faith has made you well.'

Mark 10: 46–52

An essentially biblical emphasis – all too often ignored by the Church – is that Christ is Lord and saviour of the *whole* of a man, or he is no Saviour at all. Because Jesus insisted on seeing men whole, one could never be sure which aspects of a man's needs he would tackle first. Here comes a paralysed man, helpless and obviously sick in body. His friends have brought him hoping for a simple cure, and Jesus talks about the forgiveness of his sins. Here, on the other hand, comes a clear case of spiritual need, an enquirer asking how to gain eternal life, and Jesus gives him an economic answer, telling him how to give away his goods to the poor. Because ultimately Jesus cannot rest content until *all* of a man's needs are fully met, it does not matter much to him where he starts on the work of salvation.

John V. Taylor, 'Christian Motivation in Dialogue', in
Face to Face: Essays on Inter-faith Dialogue

PRAYERS

We pray for
   the sick in body, mind or spirit
   doctors, nurses and attendants
   those who work in the social services
   hospitals, nursing homes, and medical schools

Almighty and everliving God,
whose Son Jesus Christ healed the sick
and restored them to wholeness of life:
look with compassion on the anguish of the world,
and by your healing power
make whole both men and nations;
through our Lord and Saviour Jesus Christ
who is alive and reigns with you and the Holy Spirit,
one God now and for ever.

Our Father

Come to me, all of you who are tired from carrying your heavy loads, and I will give you rest.

Who can overcome the world? Only the man who believes that Jesus is the Son of God.

1 John 5: 5

PSALM

Have mercy on me, O God, in your enduring goodness:
according to the fullness of your compassion
blot out my offences.

Wash me thoroughly from my wickedness:
and cleanse me from my sin.

For I acknowledge my rebellion:
and my sin is ever before me.

Against you only I have sinned and done that which is evil in
your eyes:
so you will be just in your sentence and blameless in your
judging.

Create me a clean heart, O God:
and renew a right spirit within me.

Do not cast me out from your presence:
do not take your holy spirit from me.

Psalm 51 (50): 1–4. 10–11

BIBLE READING

Jesus came from Nazareth, in the region of Galilee, and John baptized him in the Jordan. As soon as Jesus came up out of the water he saw heaven opening and the Spirit coming down on him, like a dove. And a voice came from heaven, 'You are my own dear Son. I am well pleased with you.' At once the Spirit made him go into the desert. He was there forty days, being tempted by Satan. Wild animals were there also, but angels came and helped him.

Mark 1: 9–13

Christ who from the beginning of his life taught by word and example, spent forty days and forty nights in prayer and fasting before he undertook his mission. He inaugurated his public ministry with the joyful message: The Kingdom of God is at hand. But he immediately added the command: Repent and believe the Good News. These words are, as it were, an epitome of the entire Christian life.

When a man encounters Christ, he is illumined by a new light and recognizes the sanctity of God and the malice of sin. Through Christ's word the call to conversion and the offer of forgiveness are made to him. These graces are fully attained in baptism, which forms a man into the likeness of the Lord's passion, death and resurrection, so that his whole life bears the imprint of the paschal mystery.

Whoever calls himself a Christian must therefore follow his Master in denying himself, carrying his cross and sharing in the sufferings of Christ. In this way he will be shaped into the pattern of the Lord's death, and so be able to share his risen glory.

From the Constitution *Poenitemini* of Pope Paul VI

PRAYERS

We pray for
    delinquents and outcasts of society
    those who work to heal men's bodies
    those who work to heal men's minds
    spiritual directors and counsellors

Almighty and everlasting God,
you hate nothing that you have made
and forgive the sins of all those who are penitent.
Create and make in us new and contrite hearts,
that, lamenting our sins and acknowledging our wretchedness,
we may receive from you, the God of all mercy,
perfect forgiveness and peace;
through Jesus Christ our Lord.

Our Father

Who can overcome the world? Only the man who believes that Jesus is the Son of God.

Lent: Monday

Jesus can help those who are tempted, because he himself was tempted and suffered.

Hebrews 2: 18

POEM *A Prayer for Recollection*

How my thoughts betray me!
   How they flit and stray!
Well they may appal me
   On great judgement day.

Through the psalms they wander
   Roads that are not right;
Mitching, shouting, squabbling
   In God's very sight.

Christ the chaste, the cherished,
   Searcher of the soul,
Grant the seven-fold spirit
   Keep them in control.

Grant me, Christ, to reach you,
   With you let me be
Who are not frail or fickle
   Nor feeble-willed like me.

Anon.

BIBLE READING

The word of God is alive and active. It is sharper than any double-edged sword, it cuts all the way through, to where soul and spirit meet, to where joints and marrow come together. It judges the desires and thoughts of men's hearts. There is nothing that can be hid from God. Everything in all creation is exposed and lies open before his eyes, and it is to him that we must all give account of ourselves. Let us, then, hold firmly to the faith we profess. For we have a great high priest who has gone into the very presence of God – Jesus, the Son of God. Our high priest is not one who cannot feel sympathy with our weaknesses. On the contrary, we have a high priest who was tempted in every way that we are, but did not sin. Let us be brave, then, and come forward to God's throne, where there is grace. There we will receive mercy and find grace to help us just when we need it.

Hebrews 4: 12-16

Abbot Pastor said that Abbot John the Dwarf had prayed to the Lord and the Lord had taken away all his passions, so that he became impossible. And in this condition he went to one of the elders and said: You see before you a man who is completely at rest and has no more temptations. The elder said: Go and pray to the Lord to command some struggle to be stirred up in you, for the soul is matured only in battles. And when the temptations started up again he did not pray that the struggle be taken away from him, but only said: Lord give me strength to get through the fight.

Thomas Merton, *The Wisdom of the Desert*

PRAYERS

We pray
   for those who suffer temptation
   that we may be preserved from falling into temptation
   that we may not lead others into wrongdoing
   that we may help others to overcome temptation

Almighty God,
whose Son Jesus Christ fasted forty days
   in the wilderness,
and was tempted as we are,
   yet without sin:
give us grace to discipline ourselves
   in submission to your Spirit;
and, as you know our weakness,
so may we know your power to save;
through Jesus Christ our Lord.

Our Father

Jesus can help those who are tempted, because he himself was tempted and suffered.

Lent: Tuesday

Your Father already knows what you need before you ask him.

Matthew 6: 8

POEM *Prayer*

Prayer, the Church's banquet, Angels' age,
    God's breath in man returning to his birth,
    The soul in paraphrase, heart in pilgrimage,
The Christian plummet, sounding heaven and earth;
Engine against the Almighty. sinner's tower,
    Reversèd thunder, Christ-side-piercing spear,
    The six-days' world transposing in an hour,
A kind of tune, which all things hear and fear;
Softness, and peace, and joy, and love, and bliss,
    Exalted manna, gladness of the best,
    Heaven in ordinary, man well drest,
The milky way, the bird of Paradise,
    Church-bells beyond the stars heard, the soul's blood,
    The land of spices; something understood.

George Herbert

BIBLE READING

Jesus said, 'Suppose one of you should go to a friend's house at midnight and tell him, "Friend, let me borrow three loaves of bread. A friend of mine who is on a journey has just come to my house and I haven't got any food for him!" And suppose your friend should answer from inside, "Don't bother me! The door is already locked, and my children and I are in bed. I can't get up to give you anything." Well, what then? I tell you, even if he will not get up and give you the bread because he is your friend, yet he will get up and give you everything you need because you are not ashamed to keep on asking. And so I say to you: Ask, and you will receive; seek, and you will find; knock, and the door will be opened to you. For everyone who asks will receive, and he who seeks will find, and the door will be opened to him who knocks'.

Luke 11: 5–10

When a child wants to talk to his father he does not make use of a manual of etiquette or a code of manners: he speaks in a simple and unaffected way, without formality; and we must do the same with our heavenly Father. He himself said: Unless you become as little children you shall not enter the kingdom of heaven. A mother never grows tired of hearing her little one say: 'Mother, I love you'. It is the same with God. The more childlike our prayer, the more it is pleasing to him. After all it was he who chose for himself the name of *Father*. Our prayer, then, must be quite simple, as simple as possible. All we have to do is to place ourselves on our knees and with complete sincerity make our acts of faith, hope and love. There is no method of prayer more certain, more elevated and more salutary than this.

A Carthusian, *The Prayer of Love and Silence*

PRAYERS

We pray for
  the Church
  religious communities
  prayer groups
  Christians living in lonely and isolated places

Almighty and everlasting God,
you are always more ready to hear than we to pray
and give more than either we desire or deserve.
Pour down upon us the abundance of your mercy,
forgiving us those things of which our conscience is afraid
and giving us those good things which we are not worthy to ask
save through the merits and mediation
  of Jesus Christ your Son our Lord.

Our Father

Your Father already knows what you need before you ask him.

Lent: Wednesday

God, be merciful to me, a sinner.

Luke 18: 13

PSALM

Out of the depths have I called to you, O Lord:
Lord, hear my voice;

O let your ears consider well:
the voice of my supplication.

If you, Lord, should note what we do wrong:
who then, O Lord, could stand?

And there is forgiveness with you:
so that you shall be feared.

I wait for the Lord; my soul waits for him:
and in his word is my hope.

O Israel, trust in the Lord, for with the Lord there is mercy:
and with him is ample redemption.

Psalm 130 (129): 1–5.7

BIBLE READING

Jesus said, 'Two men went up to the Temple to pray, one a
Pharisee, the other a tax collector. The Pharisee stood there and
said this prayer to himself, "I thank you, God, that I am not
grasping, unjust, adulterous like the rest of mankind, and particularly that I am not like this tax collector here. I fast twice a week;
I pay tithes on all I get". The tax collector stood some distance
away, not daring even to raise his eyes to heaven; but he beat his
breast and said, "God, be merciful to me, a sinner." This man, I
tell you, went home again at rights with God; the other did not.
For everyone who exalts himself will be humbled, but the man
who humbles himself will be exalted'.

Luke 18: 10–14

The tax collector, with all his faults and follies, has thought only for God; and because his mind is on God, he knows himself to be a sinner. He has lived a disreputable life, and can find no help for his condition but in God; and he finds also that such honest humility is the one sure way into the divine presence. He rather than the Pharisee is justified, declared righteous; not that he is good and the other bad – this is not the case – but because he has done the one thing that God requires of those who seek access to him: he has faced the truth about himself and cast himself on God's compassion. Whether his repentance was deep or shallow we are not told; God can use even the first traces of a nascent faith.

G. B. Caird, *Saint Luke*

PRAYERS

We pray for
    the lonely and the unloved
    the underprivileged
    those who oppress others
    those who are intolerant of others

Almighty God,
you know us to be set in the midst
    of so many and great dangers,
that, because of the frailty of our nature,
    we cannot always stand upright.
Give us such strength and protection
as may support us in all dangers
and carry us through all temptations;
through Jesus Christ our Lord.

Our Father

God, be merciful to me, a sinner.

Lent: Thursday

Since God has loved us so much, we too should love one another.

1 John 4: 11

HYMN *The Divine Image*

To Mercy, Pity, Peace, and Love
All pray in their distress;
And to these virtues of delight,
Return their thankfulness.

For Mercy, Pity, Peace, and Love
Is God, our father dear,
And Mercy, Pity, Peace, and Love
Is man, his child and care.

For Mercy has a human heart,
Pity a human face,
And Love, the human form divine,
And Peace, the human dress.

William Blake

BIBLE READING

Jesus said, 'You have heard that it was said, "Love your friends, hate your enemies". But I tell you: love your enemies, and pray for those who persecute you, so that you will become the sons of your Father in heaven. For he makes his sun to shine on bad and good people alike, and gives rain to those who do good and those who do evil. Why should God reward you if you love only the people who love you? Even the tax collectors do that! And if you speak only to your friends, have you done anything out of the ordinary? Even the pagans do that! You must be perfect – just as your Father in heaven is perfect'.

Matthew 5: 43–8

Even the night should not interrupt your works of mercy. Never say, 'Come back again, I will give you something tomorrow'. Let us carry out our good deeds immediately. Kindness is the one thing that needs no second thoughts. 'Share your bread with the poor and open your doors to the homeless', and do it with a good will. 'If you give to charity', says St Paul, 'give cheerfully', for willingness will double the effect of your good deeds. How insulting, how ungracious it would be to give reluctantly or under duress!

So then let us go about our good works in a joyful spirit, not with a face of woe. If in the words of Scripture we 'loose the bonds of those who stretch out their hands to us' or as I interpret this text, if our charity is not mean and suspicious, full of doubts and grumblings, what then? Our reward will indeed be great and wonderful.

St Gregory Nazianzen, *A Sermon on the Love of the Poor*

PRAYERS

We pray for
  the peace of the world
  young and under-developed countries
  the United Nations Organization
  those on Voluntary Service overseas

Lord, you have taught us
that all our doings without love
  are nothing worth.
Send your Holy Spirit
and pour into our hearts
  that most excellent gift of love,
the true bond of peace and of all virtues,
without which whoever lives is counted dead before you.
Grant this for the sake of your only Son,
Christ our Lord.

Our Father

Since God has loved us so much, we too should love one another.

Lent: Friday

Forgive your neighbour the hurt he does you, and when you pray,
your sins will be forgiven. Ecclesiasticus 28: 2

POEM *At a Calvary near the Ancre*

One ever hangs where shelled roads part.
　　In this war He too lost a limb,
But His disciples hide apart;
　　And now the soldiers bear with Him.

Near Golgotha strolls many a priest,
　　And in their faces there is pride,
That they were flesh-marked by the Beast
　　By whom the gentle Christ's denied.

The scribes on all the people shove
　　And bawl allegiance to the state,
But they who love the greater love
　　Lay down their life; they do not hate.

Wilfred Owen

BIBLE READING

Resentment and anger, these are foul things too,
and both are found with the sinner.
He who exacts vengeance will experience the vengeance of the
　　Lord,
who keeps strict account of sin.
Forgive your neighbour the hurt he does you,
and when you pray your sins will be forgiven.
If a man nurses anger against another,
can he then demand compassion from the Lord?
Showing no pity for a man like himself,
can he then plead for his own sins?
Mere creature of flesh, he cherishes resentment;
who will forgive him his sins?
Remember the last things and stop hating,
remember dissolution and death, and live by the command-
　　ments.
Remember the commandments and do not bear your neighbour
　　ill-will;
remember the covenant of the Most High, and overlook the
　　offence.

Ecclesiasticus 27: 30–28: 9

In the Christian faith man discovers his humanity in the fact that in spite of his inhumanity he has already been loved by God, and in spite of his faults he has already been called to the likeness of God, and in spite of all the kingdoms of the world, has been taken into the fellowship of the Son of Man. Love makes a loved being of an unloved being. The call of another makes of a desolate life a responsive life . . . In spite of Auschwitz and Hiroshima and thalidomide children, (man) can remain true to the earth, because upon this earth the cross of Christ stands. In the midst of the unbearable story of the passion of the world he discovers the reconciling story of the passion of Christ. This gives him the power to hope when there is nothing more to hope for, and to love, when he hates himself . . . Who puts him in this position? The recognition that God has made our fate and our guilt his own in the way of Jesus, the recognition that the future of man has already begun in the crucified Son of Man, reconciles man and liberates him from pride and anxiety, which have always been the sources of idolatry. This freedom we call faith.

J. Moltmann, *Man*

PRAYERS

We pray for
    those engaged in commerce and industry
    good relations between employers and employed
    trades unions
    the unemployed

Almighty and everlasting God,
who in your tender love towards mankind
    sent your Son our Saviour Jesus Christ
to take upon him our flesh
and to suffer death upon the cross,
that all mankind should follow the example of his great
    humility:
grant that we may both follow the example of his passion
and also be made partakers of his resurrection;
through Jesus Christ our Lord.

Our Father

Forgive your neighbour the hurt he does you, and when you pray, your sins will be forgiven.

Lent: Saturday

Be careful that no one among you has a heart so bad and unbelieving that he will turn away from the living God.

Hebrews 3: 12

PSALM

In God alone is my soul at rest;
my help comes from him.
He alone is my rock, my stronghold,
my fortress: I stand firm.

How long will you all attack one man
to break him down,
as though he were a tottering wall,
or a tumbling fence?

In God alone be at rest, my soul;
for my hope comes from him.
He alone is my rock, my stronghold,
my fortress: I stand firm.

Psalm 62 (61): 2–4. 6–7

BIBLE READING

Finally brothers, we urge you and appeal to you in the Lord Jesus to make more and progress in the kind of life you are meant to live; the life that God wants, as you learnt from us and as you are already living it. You have not forgotten the instructions we gave you in the authority of the Lord Jesus Christ.

What God wants is for all of you to be holy. He wants you to keep away from fornication and each one of you to know how to use the body that belongs to him in a way that is holy and honourable, not giving way to selfish lusts like the pagans who do not know God . . . We have been called by God to be holy, not to be immoral; in other words, anyone who objects is not objecting to a human authority, but to God who gives you his Holy Spirit.

1 Thessalonians 4: 1–5. 7–8

God's gift of relationship with him
and with one another,
with all that it promises of fulfilment,
is denied us by our sin.
We can understand this sin as being our assertion
that we are sufficient of ourselves,
that we do not need relationship with God or man.
We fear men and hurt them
and exploit not only persons but things.
Indeed, the worst hurt any of us can experience
is the hurt suffered at the hands
of someone we love and from whom we expect love.
Personal hurts hurt on the inside;
the others hurt on the outside.
Inside hurts are more injurious
than outside ones because
we are dependent on one another;
and when we have been hurt by another person,
there is the feeling that we have been
cut off from him, with the consequent anxiety
that to a greater or lesser extent
we will cease to be.

Ruel L. Howe, The Hurt of Sin

PRAYERS

We pray for
the sick and suffering
permanent invalids
the dying
doctors, nurses and medical students

Almighty God,
whose most dear Son went not up to joy
but first he suffered pain
and entered not into glory
before he was crucified:
grant that we, walking in the way of the cross,
may find it to be the way of life and peace;
through Jesus Christ our Lord.

Our Father

Be careful that no one among you has a heart so bad and unbelieving that he will turn away from the living God.

Maundy Thursday

Do this as a memorial of me.

1 Corinthians 11: 24

PSALM

How can I repay the Lord
for his goodness to me?
The cup of salvation I will raise;
I will call on the Lord's name.

My vows to the Lord I will fulfil
before all his people.
O precious in the eyes of the Lord
is the death of his faithful.

Your servant, Lord, your servant am I;
you have loosened my bonds.
A thanksgiving sacrifice I make:
I will call on the Lord's name.

Psalm 116 (115): 12–17

BIBLE READING

The tradition which I handed on to you came to me from the
Lord himself: that the Lord Jesus, on the night of his arrest,
took bread and, after giving thanks to God, broke it and said:
'This is my body, which is for you; do this as a memorial of me.'
In the same way, he took the cup after supper, and said: 'This
cup is the new covenant sealed by my blood. Whenever you
drink it, do this as a memorial of me.' For every time you eat this
bread and drink the cup, you proclaim the death of the Lord,
until he comes.

1 Corinthians 11: 23–6

At the heart of it all is the eucharistic action, a thing of an absolute simplicity – the taking, blessing, breaking and giving of bread and the taking, blessing and giving of a cup of wine and water, as these were first done with their new meaning by a young Jew before and after supper with His friends on the night before He died . . . He had told His friends to do this henceforward with the new meaning 'for the *remembrance*' of Him, and they have done it always since.

Was ever another command so obeyed? For century after century, spreading slowly to every continent and country and among every race on earth, this action has been done, in every conceivable circumstance, for every conceivable human need from infancy and before it to extreme old age and after it, from the pinnacles of earthly greatness to the refuge of fugitives in the caves and dens of the earth.

Dom Gregory Dix, *The Shape of the Liturgy*

PRAYERS

We pray
    for those who are physically and spiritually hungry
    that we may help to meet the needs of others
    for all agencies of relief

Almighty and heavenly Father,
we thank you that
in this wonderful sacrament
you have given us the memorial
of the passion of your Son Jesus Christ.
Grant us to reverence
the sacred mysteries of his body and blood,
that our lives may bear abundantly the fruits of his
    redemption;
who is alive and reigns with you and the Holy Spirit,
one God, now and for ever.

Our Father

Do this as a memorial of me.

Good Friday

Christ offered one sacrifice for sins, an offering that is good forever.

Hebrews 10: 12

PSALM

O God, save me by your name;
by your power, uphold my cause.
O God, hear my prayer;
listen to the words of my mouth.

For proud men have risen against me,
ruthless men seek my life.
They have no regard for God.

But I have God for my help.
The Lord upholds my life.

I will sacrifice to you with willing heart
and praise your name for it is good:
for you have rescued me from all my distress
and my eyes have seen the downfall of my foes.

Psalm 54 (53): 3–6. 8–9

BIBLE READING

It was about twelve o'clock when the sun stopped shining and darkness covered the whole country until three o'clock; and the curtain hanging in the temple was torn in two. Jesus cried out in a loud voice, 'Father! In your hands I place my spirit!' He said this and died. The army officer saw what had happened, and he praised God, saying, 'Certainly he was a good man!' When the people who had gathered there to watch the spectacle saw what happened, they all went back home, beating their breasts. All those who knew Jesus personally, including the women who had followed him from Galilee, stood off at a distance to see these things.

Luke 23: 44–9

When Christians meet together Sunday by Sunday, and supremely on Easter Day, to break bread and to share the cup over which Jesus agonized the night before he died, this is what they are affirming – that the truth about his death is the truth about their lives. And this is not because they themselves are determined to make it so, for they will often fail miserably. It is because, underlying what they hope for and despair of in themselves, they are assured that once and for all the case for love has been made and won.

For some weeks now, as I write this, the fans have been listening to a pop singer telling them: 'That's what love will do'. By the time Good Friday comes, he may have been dropped from the Top Ten. But the man on the cross will continue to affirm that same theme – though with infinitely richer power to transform and heal. For, despite what we know in ourselves and see in the world around us, '*That's* what love will do'.

J. A. T. Robinson, *But That I Can't Believe*

PRAYERS

We pray for
    victims of cruelty and persecution
    those who suffer for the sake of truth
    the lonely and the unloved

Almighty Father,
look with mercy on this your family
for which our Lord Jesus Christ
    was content to be betrayed
    and given up into the hands of wicked men
    and to suffer death upon the cross;
who is alive and glorified
with you and the Holy Spirit,
one God, now and for ever.

Our Father

Christ offered one sacrifice for sins, an offering that is good forever.

Easter Eve

Christ was put to death physically, but made alive spiritually.

1 Peter 3: 18

PSALM

The Lord is my shepherd:
therefore can I lack nothing.

He will make me lie down in green pastures:
and lead me beside still waters.

He will refresh my soul:
and guide me in right pathways for his name's sake.

Though I walk through the valley of the shadow of death, I
    will fear no evil:
for you are with me, your rod and your staff comfort me.

You spread a table before me in the face of those who trouble
    me:
you have anointed my head with oil, and my cup will be full.

Surely your goodness and loving-kindness will follow me all the
    days of my life:
And I shall dwell in the house of the Lord for ever.

Psalm 23 (22)

BIBLE READING

Jesus said to the Jews, 'Tear down this house of God and in
three days I will build it again'. 'You are going to build it again
in three days?' they asked him. 'It has taken forty-six years to
build this temple!' But the temple Jesus spoke of was his body.
So when he was raised from death, his disciples remembered that
he said this; and they believed the scripture and what Jesus had
said.

John 2: 19–22

In the history of the world, only one tomb has ever had a rock rolled before it, and a soldier guard set to watch it to prevent the dead man within from rising: that was the tomb of Christ on the evening of the Friday called Good. What spectacle could be more ridiculous than armed soldiers keeping their eyes on a corpse? They said He was dead; they knew He was dead; they would say He would not rise again; and yet they watched. They openly called Him a deceiver. But would He still deceive? . . .

Early on Saturday morning, therefore, the chief priests and the Pharisees broke the Sabbath and presented themselves to Pilate, saying: 'Give orders that His tomb shall be securely guarded until the third day' . . . Pilate said to them: 'You have guards; away with you, make it secure as you best know how.'

The watch was to prevent violence; the seal was to prevent fraud. There must be a seal, and the enemies would seal it. There must be a watch, and the enemies must keep it. The certificates of the death and resurrection must be signed by the enemies themselves.

Fulton J. Sheen, *Life of Christ*

PRAYERS

Lord God our Father,
through our Saviour Jesus Christ
you have assured mankind of eternal life
and in baptism have made us one with him.
Deliver us from the death of sin
and raise us to new life in your love,
by the grace of our Lord Jesus Christ,
in the fellowship of the Holy Spirit.

Grant, Lord,
that we who are baptized into the death
    of your Son our Saviour Jesus Christ
may continually put to death our evil desires
    and be buried with him;
that through the grave and gate of death
we may pass to our joyful resurrection,
through his merits, who died and was buried
    and rose again for us,
your Son Jesus Christ our Lord.

Our Father

Christ was put to death physically, but made alive spiritually.

Easter: Sunday

Christ is risen. Alleluia!

CANTICLE

Christ our passover has been sacrificed for us:
so let us celebrate the feast,
not with the old leaven of corruption and wickedness:
but with the unleavened bread of sincerity and truth.

Christ once raised from the dead dies no more:
In dying he died to sin once for all:
in living he lives to God.
See yourselves therefore as dead to sin:
and alive to God in Jesus Christ our Lord.

The Easter Anthems 1–5

BIBLE READING

After the sabbath, and towards dawn on the first day of the week, Mary of Magdala and the other Mary went to visit the sepulchre. And all at once there was a violent earthquake, for the angel of the Lord, descending from heaven, came and rolled away the stone and sat on it. His face was like lightning, his robe white as snow. The guards were so shaken, so frightened of him, that they were like dead men. But the angel spoke; and he said to the women, 'There is no need for you to be afraid. I know you are looking for Jesus, who was crucified. He is not here, he is risen, as he said he would. Come and see the place where he lay, then go quickly and tell his disciples, He has risen from the dead and now he is going before you into Galilee; it is there you will see him. Now I have told you.' Filled with awe and great joy the women came quickly away from the tomb and ran to tell the disciples.

Matthew 28: 1–8

If it is said: He has overcome and swallowed death, broken the chains of the devil and destroyed his power, this is so; it is accomplished, it is finished. After Christ's resurrection death is no more, nor does sin rule. Death and sin *do* continue to exist, but are vanquished things. Their situation is similar to a chess player who has already lost but has not acknowledged it as yet. He looks at the game and says: 'Is it over already? Doesn't the king have one other move?' He tries it and afterwards admits that there was no chance of winning.

The old era, the time of death and sin is over and the game only appears to be carrying on. 'Old things have passed away, behold all things are made new' (2 Cor. 5: 17).

Such is Easter or else it is nothing at all. You may say: at heart nothing has changed since Easter, people die, they fight each other and sin, the devil is as active as ever. But in the light of Easter this idea reveals itself as the great illusion, the sad human illusion. You should realize the falsity of this notion, for the belief that still views death and sin as victorious powers is simply a myth. The demon's chains have been broken. This is the truth.

Karl Barth, *The Faith of the Church*

PRAYERS

We praise God that the risen Christ is present with us.
We pray for
   those who speak and act in his name
   those who stand firm in the faith in difficulty and persecution

Lord of all life and power,
through the mighty resurrection of your Son
you have overcome the old order of sin and death
and have made all things new in him.
Grant that we, being dead to sin
and alive to you in Jesus Christ,
may reign with him in glory;
to whom with you and the Holy Spirit
be praise and honour, glory and might,
now and in all eternity.

Our Father

Christ is risen. Alleluia!

You are to think of yourselves as dead to sin but alive to God in union with Christ Jesus.

Romans 6: 11

HYMN *Sing to Christ the Lord*

Sing to Christ the Lord, Our Lord who has risen in glory,
Risen to life anew, breaking the kingdom of death.

Lo, the fair beauty of earth, from the death of the winter
  arising,
Every good gift of the year now to its Master returns.

He who was nailed to the Cross is God and the Ruler of all
  things,
All things created on earth worship the Maker of all.

Sing to Christ the Lord, Our Lord who has risen in glory,
Risen to life anew, breaking the kingdom of death.

Venantius Fortunatus

BIBLE READING

For if we became one with him in dying as he did, in the same way we shall be one with him by being raised to life as he was. And we know this: our old being has been put to death with Christ on his cross, in order that the power of the sinful self might be destroyed, so that we should no longer be the slaves of sin. For when a person dies he is set free from the power of sin. If we have died with Christ, we believe that we will also live with him. For we know that Christ has been raised from death and will never die again – death has no more power over him. The death he died was death to sin, once and for all; and the life he now lives is life to God. In the same way you are to think of yourselves as dead to sin but alive to God in union with Christ Jesus.

Romans 6: 5–11

Due to my involvement in the struggle
    for the freedom of my people,
I have known very few quiet days
    in the last few years.
I have been arrested five times
    and put in Alabama jails.
My home has been bombed twice.
    A day seldom passes that my family and I
are not recipients of threats of death.
    I have been the victim of near-fatal stabbing.
So in a real sense I have been battered
    by the storms of persecution.
I must admit that at times I have felt
    that I could no longer bear such a heavy burden,
and have been tempted to retreat
    to a more quiet and serene life.
But every time such a temptation appeared,
    something came to strengthen my determination.
I have learned now that the Master's burden is light
    precisely when we take his yoke upon us.

                Martin Luther King, *Strength to Love*

PRAYERS

We pray for
    those who bear witness to the risen Christ in commerce and
        industry
    chaplains to the forces
    those who preserve law and order

Almighty Father,
who in your great mercy make glad the disciples
    with the sight of the risen Lord:
give us such knowledge of his presence with us,
that we may be strengthened and sustained by his risen life
and serve you continually in righteousness and truth;
through Jesus Christ our Lord.

Our Father

You are to think of yourselves as dead to sin but alive to God in
union with Christ Jesus.

Easter: Tuesday

The Lord is risen indeed! He has appeared to Simon!

Luke 24: 34

CANTICLE *Glory and honour*

Glory and honour and power:
are yours by right, O Lord our God;
For you created all things:

and by your will they have their being.
Glory and honour and power:
are yours by right, O Lamb who was slain;
For by your blood you ransomed men for God:
from every race and language, from every people and nation,
to make them a kingdom of priests:
to stand and serve before our God.

To him who sits on the throne, and to the Lamb:
be praise and honour, glory and might for ever and ever. Amen.

BIBLE READING

Peter said, 'You know of the great event that took place throughout all the land of Israel, beginning in Galilee, after the baptism
that John preached. You know about Jesus of Nazareth, how
God poured out on him the Holy Spirit and power. He went
everywhere, doing good and healing all who were under the
power of the Devil, because God was with him. We are witnesses
of all that he did in the country of the Jews and in Jerusalem.
They put him to death by nailing him to the cross. But God
raised him from death on the third day, and caused him to
appear, not to all the people, but only to us who are the witnesses
that God had already chosen. We ate and drank with him after
he rose from death. And he commanded us to preach the gospel
to the people, and to testify that he is the one whom God has
appointed judge of the living and the dead.'

Acts 10: 37–43

The early Christian community understood Jesus as 'He who leads to life' and as 'the Principle of a new world.' All the experiences of life, including suffering and death, can be fitted into this basic attitude. In this way something radically new enters our world, new styles of patience, endurance, understanding. God wants to set us free from the grip of routine and dullness. Not simply to experience joy, but to *be joy* is the costing task of every fresh day. But true joy can only be found where joy is given to others. Since the resurrection of Jesus Christ the true test of our Christian existence is the selfless gift of joy to others. In this way every man, whether baptized or not, can experience in his whole being a foretaste of heaven. And so the Christian's task is to let the light of heaven shine through human experience, so that it becomes transparent.

Ladislaus Boros, *Breaking through to God*

PRAYERS

We pray for
    those who teach and preach the Christian faith
    theological colleges and institutions
    school children and students

God of peace,
who brought again from the dead our Lord Jesus Christ,
that great shepherd of the sheep,
by the blood of the eternal covenant:
make us perfect in every good work to do your will,
and work in us that which is well-pleasing in your sight;
through Jesus Christ our Lord.

Our Father

The Lord is risen indeed! He has appeared to Simon!

Easter: Wednesday

They told how they had recognized Jesus at the breaking of bread. Luke 24: 35

POEM *Love*

Love bade me welcome; yet my soul drew back,
    Guilty of dust and sin.
But quick-eyed Love, observing me grow slack
    From my first entrance in,
Drew nearer to me, sweetly questioning,
    If I lacked anything.

'A guest', I answered, 'worthy to be here'.
    Love said, 'You shall be he?'
'I, the unkind, ungrateful? Ah, my dear,
    I cannot look on thee.'
Love took my hand, and smiling did reply,
    'Who made the eyes but I?'

'Truth, Lord, but I have marred them; let my shame
    Go where it doth deserve.'
'And know you not', says Love, 'who bore the blame?'
    'My dear, then I will serve.'
'You must sit down', says Love, 'and taste my meat'.
    So I did sit and eat.

George Herbert

BIBLE READING

That very same day, two of them were on their way to a village called Emmaus, seven miles from Jerusalem, and they were talking about all that had happened. Now as they talked this over, Jesus himself came up and walked by their side, but something prevented them from recognizing him. He said to them, 'What matters are you discussing as you walk along?' They stopped short, their faces downcast.

When they drew near to the village to which they were going, he made as if to go on; but they pressed him to stay with them. 'It is nearly evening', they said, 'and the day is almost over'. So he went in to stay with them. Now while he was with them at table, he took the bread and said the blessing, then he broke it and handed it to them. And their eyes were opened and they recognized him; but he had vanished from their sight'.

Luke 24: 13–17. 28–32

To say that the Easter observances are the centre of the ecclesiastical year leaves much untold; they are the centre where all the liturgy converges and the spring whence it all flows. All Christian worship is but a continuous celebration of Easter: the sun, rising and setting daily, leaves in its wake an uninterrupted series of Eucharists; every mass that is celebrated prolongs the pasch. Each day of the liturgical year, and within each day, every instant of the sleepless life of the Church, continues and renews the pasch that Our Lord had desired with such great desire to eat with his disciples while awaiting the pasch. He should eat in His kingdom the pasch to be prolonged for all eternity. The annual pasch, which we are constantly recalling or anticipating, preserves us ever in the sentiment of the early Christians, who exclaimed, looking to the past, 'The Lord is risen indeed,' and, turning towards the future, 'Come, Lord Jesus! Come! Make no delay.'

L. Bouyer, *The Paschal Mystery*

PRAYERS

We pray for
   farmers and fishermen
   those engaged in the making and distribution of food
   agencies of relief
   the hungry

Almighty God,
whose Son Jesus Christ is the resurrection and the life
   of all who put their trust in him:
raise us, we pray, from the death of sin
   to the life of righteousness;
that we may seek the things which are above,
where he reigns with you and the Holy Spirit,
one God, now and for ever.

Our Father

They told how they had recognized Jesus at the breaking of bread.

Easter: Thursday

As in Adam all die, so also in Christ shall all be made alive.

1 Corinthians 15: 20

PSALM

How great is your name, O Lord our God,
through all the earth!
Your majesty is praised above the heavens;
on the lips of children and of babes
you have found praise to foil your enemy,
to silence the foe and the rebel.

When I see the heavens the work of your hands,
the moon and the stars which you arranged,
what is man that you should keep him in mind,
mortal man that you care for him?

Yes you have made him little less than a god;
with glory and honour you crowned him,
gave him power over the work of your hands,
put all things under his feet.

Psalm 8: 1–7

BIBLE READING

What is made of flesh and blood cannot share in God's Kingdom,
and what is mortal cannot possess immortality. Listen to this
secret: we shall not all die, but in an instant we shall all be
changed, as quickly as the blinking of an eye, when the last
trumpet sounds. For when it sounds, the dead will be raised
immortal beings, and we shall all be changed. For what is mortal
must clothe itself with what cannot die. So when what is mortal
has been clothed with what is immortal, and when what will die
has been clothed with what cannot die, then the scripture will
come true: 'Death is destroyed; victory is complete!'

'Where, Death, is your victory? Where, Death, is your power
to hurt?' Death gets its power to hurt from sin, and sin gets its
power from the law. But thanks be to God who gives us the
victory through our Lord Jesus Christ!

1 Corinthians 15: 50–7

Only in spiritual and religious combat can death be conquered. In itself death is a factor in the general decay, dissolution, corruption and ruin. Only Christ succeeded in conquering it and transforming it into a mystery of life and resurrection. Since God's son became a man among men and resolved to share our mortal condition death is no longer seen as an absolute and utter evil. Christ's death has freed us from subjection to a meaningless and hopeless doom; it has become a mysterious transformation, a passage from one life to another. Consequently it has lost its absolute character and become part of the general mystery of life, indeed one of its most decisive moments. It is no longer anything but an occurrence, but one of supreme significance.

Ignace Lepp, *The Challenges of Life*

PRAYERS

We pray for
the aged and the dying
those suffering from incurable illnesses
the maimed and crippled
those who minister to them

God our Father,
look upon us with love.
You redeem us and make us your children in Christ.
Give us true freedom
and bring us to the inheritance you promised.
We ask this through Christ our Lord.

Our Father

As in Adam all die, so also in Christ shall all be made alive.

Easter Friday:

Let us be concerned with one another, to help one another to show love and do good.

Hebrews 10: 24

POEM *Easter*

Most glorious Lord of life, that on this day
    Didst make thy triumph over death and sin;
    And having harrowed hell didst bring away
    Captivity thence captive, us to win:
This joyous day, dear Lord, with joy begin,
    And grant that we for whom thou didst die
    Being with thy dear blood clean washed from sin,
    May live forever in felicity.
And that thy love we weighing worthily,
    May likewise love thee for the same again;
    And for thy sake that all like dear didst buy,
    With love may one another entertain.
So let us love, dear love, like as we ought.
Love is the lesson which the Lord us taught.

Edmund Spenser

BIBLE READING

We have complete freedom to go into the Most Holy Place by means of the death of Jesus. He opened for us a new way, a living way, through the curtain – that is, through his own body. We have a great priest in charge of the house of God. Let us come near to God, then, with a sincere heart and a sure faith, with hearts that have been made clean from a guilty conscience, and bodies washed with pure water. Let us hold on firmly to the hope we profess, because we can trust God to keep his promise. Let us be concerned with one another, to help one another to show love and to do good.

Hebrews 10: 19–24

Love the Church as the Lord Himself. Though she is burdened with the weakness and sinfulness of a long history she is still the instrument of His Kingdom, His work of salvation for the world, the germ of a new creation.

If you love the Church have a profound respect for her institutions and mission. Whatever is impure and useless in her must be healed, not attacked, and purified in suffering rather than criticized.

Give yourself time to discover this Church as a marvellously deep mystery of fellowship in faith, hope and love, transcending all barriers of time and space. Built upon the foundation of the apostles and prophets, she makes you members of the household of all God's saints.

The Church comes into being in the community where you live, not so much in her official structures as in her essential form of brotherhood and new creation.

Rule for a new Brother, Brakkenstein Community, Holland

PRAYERS

We pray for
   the unity of all Christian people
   our own Church and parish
   the community in which we live and work
   our family

God of unchanging power and light,
look with mercy and favour on your entire Church.
Bring lasting salvation to mankind,
so that the world may see
the fallen lifted up,
the old made new,
and all things brought to perfection,
through him who is their origin,
our Lord Jesus Christ,
who lives and reigns for ever and ever.

Our Father

Let us be concerned with one another, to help one another to show love and to do good.

Easter: Saturday

Victory to our God who sits on the throne, and to the Lamb!

Revelation 7: 10

CANTICLE

Salvation and glory and power belong to our God,
His judgments are true and just.
Alleluia.

Praise our God, all you his servants,
You who fear him small and great.
Alleluia.

The Lord our God, the Almighty, reigns.
Let us rejoice and exult and give him the glory,
Alleluia.

The wedding-day of the Lamb has come,
And his bride has made herself ready,
Alleluia.

Revelation 19: 1–2. 5–7

BIBLE READING

I saw a new heaven and a new earth. The first heaven and the first earth disappeared, and the sea vanished. And I saw the Holy City, the new Jerusalem, coming down out of heaven from God, prepared and ready, like a bride dressed to meet her husband. I heard a loud voice speaking from the throne, 'Now God's home is with men! He will live with them, and they shall be his people. God himself will be with them, and he will be their God'. He will wipe away all tears from their eyes. Their will be no more death, no more grief, crying, or pain. The old things have disappeared.

Revelation 21: 1–4

If Jesus came down on earth today, how would he read his newspaper? One thing I know, he would certainly read it. How could he possibly be indifferent to the world's news? . . . What would he see in the daily chain of human events which are painful, joyful, discouraging, amusing, horrifying? Would he find in these things material for discussion, or for strong emotions, or for anger? He would find all of these in them. But, beyond human events, he would see the kingdom of his Father being built or demolished . . . 'What is happening to my brothers, who are my living members?' he would ask. 'Is my Body being built up? What were the problems yesterday, the failures and the successes? What will they be today?' And, with his newspaper in his hand, Jesus would pray to the Father.

Michael Quoist, *Meet Christ and Live*

PRAYERS

We pray for
   the peace of the world
   our country
   the Queen and her government
   those in positions of responsibility

Almighty and eternal God,
you created all things in wonderful beauty and order.
Help us now to perceive
how still more wonderful is the new creation
by which in the fullness of time
you redeemed your people
through the sacrifice of our passover, Jesus Christ,
who lives and reigns for ever and ever.

Our Father

Victory to our God who sits on the throne, and to the Lamb!

Ascension

As Jesus was blessing them, he departed from them and was taken up into heaven.

Luke 24: 51

PSALM

You have gone up on high; you have taken captives,
receiving men in tribute, O God,
even those who rebel, into your dwelling, O Lord.

Kingdoms of the earth, sing to God, praise the Lord
who rides on the heavens, the ancient heavens.
He thunders his voice, his mighty voice.
Come, acknowledge the power of God.

His glory is over Israel; his might is in the skies.
God is to be feared in his holy places.
He is the Lord, Israel's God.
He gives strength and power to his people.

Blessed be God!

Psalm 68 (67): 19. 33–6

BIBLE READING

When the apostles met together with Jesus they asked him, 'Lord will you at this time give the Kingdom back to Israel?' Jesus said to them, 'The times and occasions are set by my Father's own authority, and it is not for you to know when they will be. But you will be filled with power when the Holy Spirit comes on you, and you will be witnesses for me in Jerusalem, in all of Judea and Samaria, and to the ends of the earth.' After saying this, he was taken up to heaven as they watched him; and a cloud hid him from their sight.

Acts 1: 6–9

SECOND READING

The meaning of the Ascension is that the Christian Church believes that Jesus is one with the glory of God and that his presence in its corporate and individual life is God's presence. To live by this faith must mean to find life bathed in the light of an increasing hopefulness and joy. There cannot be anything better than the presence of God, now that Jesus has shown us what he is like . . . Jesus was entirely given over to God and revealed that anyone so disposed lives a spontaneous, affectionate, honest and brave life . . . We think of Jesus and God together now, to be trusted and loved, as indeed life is to be trusted and loved because it is God's love expressed in time. All this is faith; no one knows it to be true, no one knows that it is not true.

J. Neville Ward, *Five for Sorrow, Ten for Joy*

PRAYERS

We pray for
   those who minister justice
   members of the legal profession
   the police

Almighty God,
as we believe your only-begotten Son, our Lord Jesus Christ,
   has ascended into the heavens,
so may we also in heart and mind thither ascend
and with him continually dwell;
who is alive and reigns with you and the Holy Spirit,
one God, now and for ever.

Our Father

As Jesus was blessing them, he departed from them and was taken up into heaven.

Pentecost

When the Spirit of truth comes, he will lead you into all the truth.

John 16: 13

HYMN *Fellowship in the Holy Spirit*

Filled with the Spirit's power, with one accord
the infant Church confessed its risen Lord.
O Holy Spirit, in the Church today
no less your power of fellowship display.

Now with the mind of Christ set us on fire,
that unity may be our great desire.
Give joy and peace; give faith to hear your call,
and readiness in each to work for all.

Widen our love, good Spirit, to embrace
in your strong care the men of every race.
Like wind and fire with life among us move,
till we are known as Christ's, and Christians prove.

J. R. Peacey

BIBLE READING

It was to us that God made known his secret, by means of his
Spirit. The Spirit searches everything, even the hidden depths of
God's purposes. As for a man, it is his own spirit within him that
knows all about him; in the same way, only God's Spirit knows
all about God. We have not received this world's spirit; we have
received the Spirit sent by God, so that we may know all that God
has given us. So then, we do not speak in words taught by human
wisdom, but in words taught by the Spirit, as we explain spiritual
truths to those who have the Spirit. But the man who does not
have the Spirit cannot receive the gifts that come from God's
Spirit. He really does not understand them; they are nonsense to
him, because their value can be judged only on a spiritual basis.
The man who has the Spirit is able to judge the value of everything.

1 Corinthians 2: 10–15

No institution on earth has sustained such constant attacks from without and betrayals within . . . Yet so far from showing signs of disappearing with its day, unexpected resources have again and again turned the worst moments of apparent failure into a new era of growth . . . For this survival has not been that of a fortress standing foursquare and uncaptured; but that of an army with banners, moving, advancing, ubiquitous . . . Onward it goes, not by virtue of the courage of generalship of its earthly chiefs, nor yet by the often ill-directed ardour of its warriors; but by something implicit in its nature, some irresistible yearning towards some perfect achievement and more profound interpretation, some persevering disgust with things that are; in fact by the drive of Holy Spirit.

E. Milner-White, 'The Spirit and the Church in History', in *Essays Catholic and Critical*

PRAYERS

We pray
   that all men may have the gift of the Spirit
   for all who seek and proclaim the truth
   for scholars and teachers

Almighty God,
who at this time
taught the hearts of your faithful people
by sending to them the light of your Holy Spirit:
grant us by the same Spirit
   to have a right judgment in all things,
and evermore to rejoice in his holy comfort;
through the merits of Christ Jesus our Saviour,
who is alive and reigns with you
   in the unity of the Spirit,
one God, now and for ever.

Our Father

When the Spirit of truth comes, he will lead you into the truth.

Trinity Sunday

Jesus said, 'The Counsellor, the Holy Spirit, whom the Father will send in my name, he will teach you all things, and bring to your remembrance all that I have said to you'.

John 14: 26

HYMN *Father most holy*

Father most holy, gracious and forgiving,
Christ, high exalted, prince of our salvation,
Spirit of counsel, nourishing creation,
God ever living;

Trinity blessèd, unity unshaken,
Only true Godhead, sea of bounty endless,
Light of the angels, succour thou the friendless,
Shield the forsaken.

Boundless thy praise be, whom no limit boundeth,
God in three person, high in heaven living,
Where adoration, homage and thanksgiving
Ever resoundeth.

10th century. Tr. S. A. Knox

BIBLE READING

Jesus said, 'I have much more to tell you, but now it would be too much for you to bear. But when the Spirit of truth comes, he will lead you into all the truth. He will not speak on his own, but he will speak of what he hears and tell you of things to come. He will give me glory, because he will take what I have to say and tell it to you. All that my Father has is mine; that is why I said that the Spirit will take what I give him and tell it to you'.

John 16: 12–15

I must cure myself of any tendency I may have to live as though I were myself the self-contained centre of my world, seeking to reconcile my earthly interests with my duty to the God who is a mysterious threeness in oneness above the skies. I must practise myself in substituting for this the attitude of one who is trying by the guidance of the Spirit to see the world as Christ sees it, that is, to see it as our heavenly Father's world, in which our Father's work is waiting to be found and done by those whose eyes are opened to find it . . . We look out into all the world around us as those who are being sent forth, united with Christ and enlightened by the Spirit, in order that we may share God's joy in all that is good and true and beautiful, His grief at all that is ugly and base and sinful, His labour in overcoming the evil and building up the good.

L. Hodgson, *Doctrine of the Trinity*

PRAYERS

We pray for
the unity of all Christian people
those whose faith is imperfect
those who have lost their faith
victims of ignorance

Almighty and eternal God,
you have revealed yourself as Father, Son, and Holy Spirit,
and live and reign in the perfect unity of love:
keep us steadfast in this faith,
that we may know you in all your ways
and evermore rejoice in your eternal glory,
who are three Persons in one God,
now and for ever.

Our Father

Jesus said, 'The Counsellor, the Holy Spirit, whom the Father will send in my name, he will teach you all things, and bring to your remembrance all that I have said to you.'

All will openly proclaim that Jesus Christ is the Lord, to the glory of God the Father.

Philippians 2: 11

PSALM

O sing to the Lord a new song:
sing to the Lord, all the earth.

Sing to the Lord and bless his name:
proclaim the good news of his salvation from day to day.

Declare his glory among the nations:
and his wonders among all peoples.

For great is the Lord, and greatly to be praised:
he is more to be feared than all gods.

Majesty and glory are before him:
beauty and power are in his sanctuary.

Render to the Lord, you families of the nations:
render to the Lord glory and might.

Psalm 96 (95): 1–4. 6–7

BIBLE READING

Peter said, 'Men of Israel, listen to me: I speak of Jesus of Nazareth, a man singled out by God and made known to you through miracles, portents, and signs, which God worked among you through him, as you well know. When he had been given up to you, by the deliberate will and plan of God, you used heathen men to crucify and kill him.

The Jesus we speak of has been raised by God, as we can all bear witness. Exalted thus with God's right hand, he received the Holy Spirit from the Father, as was promised, and all that you now see and hear flows from him. Let all Israel then accept as certain that God has made this Jesus, whom you crucified, both Lord and Messiah'.

Acts 2: 22–3. 32–3. 36

The kingship of God, the Lordship of God whose nearness at hand had been proclaimed by Jesus, had in fact been manifested in the world through Jesus. Therefore, so the first Christians put it, Jesus was Lord, for it was in and through Jesus that the lordship of God over all things had first been finally manifest and would be ultimately established . . . Jesus was the man of God who lived and died for the living God who would be the father of all men; and the good news which Christianity proclaims for men to accept or reject is this: that this God raised up Jesus and thus vindicated both Jesus and himself. We may be sure, therefore (such is the Gospel) that he is indeed God, is indeed Father, is indeed Lord.

D. E. Jenkins and S. B. Caird, Jesus & God

PRAYERS

We give thanks for
   the apostles and evangelists
   those who proclaim the Gospel by word and deed

We pray for
   preachers, teachers and writers
   societies who distribute the scriptures

Almighty God,
you have taught us by your word
that there is salvation in no other name than in the Name of
   Jesus.
Give us grace faithfully to bear his Name
and to proclaim him as the Saviour of all mankind;
who is alive and reigns with you and the Holy Spirit,
one God, now and for ever.

Our Father

All will openly proclaim that Jesus Christ is the Lord, to the glory of God the Father.

First Week After Pentecost: Monday

Holy Father! Keep them safe by the power of your name, the name you gave me, so they may be one just as you and I are one.

John 17: 11

PSALM

How good and how pleasant it is,
brothers dwelling in unity!

It is like precious oil upon the head
running down upon the beard,
running down upon Aaron's beard
upon the collar of his robes.

It is like the dew of Hermon which falls
on the heights of Sion.
For there the Lord gives his blessing,
life for ever.

Psalm 133 (132)

BIBLE READING

These (people) remained faithful to the teaching of the apostles, to the brotherhood, to the breaking of bread and to the prayers.

The many miracles and signs worked through the apostles made a deep impression on everyone.

The faithful all lived together and owned everything in common; they sold their goods and possessions and shared out the proceeds among themselves according to what each one needed.

They went as a body to the Temple every day but met in their houses for the breaking of bread; they shared their food gladly and generously; they praised God and were looked up to by everyone. Day by day the Lord added to their community those destined to be saved.

Acts 2: 42–7

The unity of the Church is something much more than unity of ecclesiastical structure, though it cannot be complete without this. It is the love of God in Christ possessing the hearts of men so as to unite them in itself – as the Father and the Son are united in that love of Each for Each which is the Holy Spirit . . . It is therefore something much more than a means to any end – even though that end be the evangelization of the world; it is itself the one worthy end of all human aspiration; it is the life of heaven . . .

Before the loftiness of that hope and calling our little experience of unity and fellowship is humbled to the dust . . . Let all of us . . . take note of the judgment under which we stand by virtue of the gulf separating the level of our highest attainment and noblest enterprise, from 'the prize of the call upwards which God gives in Christ Jesus' (Phil. 3: 14) – *that they may be one as we.*

W. Temple *Readings in St John's Gospel*

PRAYERS

We give thanks for
the faithful witness of all those true to Christ
the continuing presence and power of the Spirit

We pray for
the unity of all Christian people
agencies for unity

Heavenly Father,
whose Son our Lord Jesus Christ
said to his apostles,
Peace I leave with you, my peace I give to you:
regard not our sins but the faith of your Church,
and grant it that peace and unity
which is agreeable to your will:
through Jesus Christ our Lord.

Our Father

Holy Father! Keep them safe by the power of your name, the name you gave me, so they may be one just as you and I are one.

First Week After Pentecost: Tuesday

In union with Christ Jesus you are being built together with all the others into a house where God lives through his Spirit.

Ephesians 2: 22

PSALM

Lord, who shall be admitted to your tent
and dwell on your holy mountain?

He who walks without fault,
he who acts with justice
and speaks the truth from his heart;
he who does not slander with his tongue;
he who does no wrong to his brother,
who casts no slur on his neighbour,
who holds the godless in disdain,
but honours those who fear the Lord;

he who keeps his pledge, come what may;
who takes no interest on a loan
and accepts no bribes against the innocent.
Such a man will stand firm for ever.

Psalm 15 (14)

BIBLE READING

I am the real vine, and my Father is the gardener. He breaks off every branch in me that does not bear fruit, and prunes every branch that does bear fruit, so that it will be clean and bear more fruit . . . Remain united to me, and I will remain united to you. A branch cannot bear fruit by itself; it can do so only if it remains in the vine. In the same way you cannot bear fruit unless you remain in me. I am the vine, you are the branches. Whoever remains in me, and I in him, will bear much fruit; for you can do nothing without me.

John 15: 1–2. 4–5

The practical application of charity was probably the most potent single cause of Christian success. The pagan comment 'See how these Christians love one another' (reported by Tertullian) was not irony. Christian charity expressed itself in care for the poor, for widows and orphans, in visits to brethren in prison or condemned to the living death of labour in the mines, and in social action in time of calamity like famine, earthquake, pestilence, or war . . . For the Christians the *raison d'être* of the church consisted in its reconciling role for all mankind, including Jew and Gentile alike, religious and even irreligious alike . . . The paradox of the church was that it was a religious revolutionary movement, yet without a conscious political ideology; it aimed at the capture of society through all its strata, but was at the same time characteristic for its indifference to the possession of power in this world.

Henry Chadwick, *The Early Church*

PRAYERS

We pray for
    our families, friends and neighbours
    Christian congregations and communities
    the lonely and the unwanted

Almighty and everlasting God,
by whose Spirit the whole body of your faithful people is
    governed and sanctified:
hear our prayers which we offer for all members of your holy
    Church;
that each in his vocation and ministry
may serve you in holiness and truth
to the glory of your Name;
through our Lord and Saviour Jesus Christ. Amen.

Our Father

In union with Christ Jesus you are being built together with all the others into a house where God lives through his Spirit.

First Week After Pentecost: Wednesday

Believe in the Lord Jesus, and you will be saved.
Acts 16: 31

HYMN *The Glorious Work of Christ*

Glorious the day when Christ was born
to wear the crown that caesars scorn,
Whose life and death that love reveal
which all men need and need to feel.

Glorious the day when Christ arose,
the surest Friend of all his foes;
Who for the sake of those he grieves
Transcends the world he never leaves.

Glorious the days of gospel grace
When Christ restores the fallen race;
When doubters kneel and waverers stand,
and faith achieves what reason planned.

Glorious the day when Christ fulfils
What man rejects yet feebly wills;
When that strong Light puts out the sun
And all is ended, all begun.
F. Pratt Green

BIBLE READING

It was Jesus who 'gave gifts to men'; he appointed some to be apostles, others to be prophets, others to be evangelists, others to be pastors and teachers. He did this to prepare all God's people for the work of Christian service, to build up the body of Christ. And so we shall all come together to that oneness in our faith and in our knowledge of the Son of God; we shall become mature men, reaching to the very height of Christ's full stature. Then we shall no longer be children, carried by the waves and blown about by every shifting wind of the teaching of deceitful men, who lead others to error by the tricks they invent. Instead, by speaking the truth in a spirit of love, we must grow up in every way to Christ, who is the head. Under his control all the different parts of the body fit together, and the whole body is held together by every joint with which it is provided. So when each separate part works as it should, the whole body grows and builds itself up through love. Ephesians 4: 11-16

That view of man which comes to us in Jesus Christ, through his person and his work, is made present and contemporary through the church. Christ fashions a new form of his own existence in this church, living in the currents of the world and of history, and in his new existence Christ continues to work in word and sacrament . . . If the existence of this church formed from men is grounded in Christ, then the church's existence and mission implies that the church should present itself in the world and in history in such a way that every dimension of whatever is human comes into view. In other words, the church must be *catholic* in the fundamental meaning of the word: catholic, encompassing, encountering, concerned with the *oikumene*, with the entire world.

Heinrich Fries, *Aspects of the Church*

PRAYERS

We give thanks for
    those who bear faithful witness to Christ
    the continuing witness of the Church

We pray for those who try to reveal Christ's present work in
    the world

Lord God our Father,
through our Saviour Jesus Christ
you have assured mankind of eternal life
and in baptism have made us one with him.
Deliver us from the death of sin
and raise us to new life in your love,
by the grace of our Lord Jesus Christ,
in the fellowship of the Holy Spirit.

Our Father

    Believe in the Lord Jesus, and you will be saved.

Are not five sparrows sold for two farthings? And not one of them is forgotten in the sight of God.

Luke 12: 6

PSALM

I lift up my eyes to the hills:
but where shall I find help?

My help comes from the Lord:
who has made heaven and earth.

He will not suffer your foot to stumble:
and he who watches over you will not sleep.

Be sure he who has charge of Israel:
will neither slumber nor sleep.

The Lord himself is your keeper:
the Lord is your defence upon your right hand;

The sun shall not strike you by day:
nor shall the moon by night.

The Lord will defend you from all evil:
it is he who will guard your life.

The Lord will defend your going out and your coming in:
from this time forward for evermore.

Psalm 121 (120)

BIBLE READING

Jesus told this parable: 'What man of you, having a hundred sheep, if he has lost one of them does not leave the ninety-nine in the wilderness, and go after the one which is lost until he finds it? And when he has found it, he lays it on his shoulders, rejoicing. And when he comes home, he calls together his friends and his neighbours, saying to them, "Rejoice with me, for I have found my sheep which was lost". Even so, I tell you, there will be more joy in heaven over one sinner who repents than over ninety-nine righteous persons who need no repentance.

Luke 15: 3-7

I do not agree with the big way of doing things. To us what matters is an individual. To get to love the person we must come in close contact with him. If we wait till we get the numbers, then he will be lost in the numbers. And we will never be able to show that love and respect for the person. I believe in person to person; every person is Christ for me, and since there is only one Jesus, that person is only one person in the world for me at that moment . . .

We ourselves feel that what we are doing is just a drop in the ocean. But if that drop was not in the ocean I think the ocean will be less because of that missing drop.

Mother Teresa in M. Muggeridge,
Something Beautiful for God

PRAYERS

We pray for
    friends and neighbours
    the unloved and the lonely
    the aged

Almighty Father,
whose Son Jesus Christ has taught us
that what we do for the least of our brethren
    we do also for him:
give us the will to be the servant of others
    as he was the servant of all,
who gave up his life and died for us,
but is alive and reigns with you and the Holy Spirit,
one God now and for ever.

Our Father

Are not five sparrows sold for two farthings? And not one of them is forgotten in the sight of God.

First Week After Pentecost: Friday

God our Saviour wants all men to be saved and to come to know the truth.

1 Timothy 2: 4

PSALM

O praise the Lord, all nations!
O extol him, all peoples!
For great is his steadfast love toward us;
and the faithfulness of the Lord endures for ever.
Praise the Lord!

Psalm 117 (116)

BIBLE READING

The eleven disciples went to the hill in Galilee where Jesus had told them to go. When they saw him they worshipped him, even though some of them doubted. Jesus drew near and said to them, 'I have been given all authority in heaven and on earth. Go, then, to all peoples everywhere and make them my disciples: baptize them in the name of the Father, the Son, and the Holy Spirit, and teach them to obey everything I have commanded you. And remember! I will be with you always, to the end of the age'.

Matthew 28: 16–20

The universe is dense, filled and intimate, and I am at its centre,
in the love of God, and on the ladder of God's love, which rises
even beyond ecstasy. I am at the centre of God's suffering, the
heart of pain. All around me the divine machinery of evil pulses
like the plunging of pistons – cruelty, vengefulness, greed, envy,
stupidity, selfishness, arrogance. And mingled with them are
gentleness, innocence, friendship, trust, solidarity, fidelity,
mother-love and the love of lovers, charitable work, serenity of
spirit, prayer and holiness. I have been merged in the town and
the things that make the town, people, buildings and machines,
all the devices of civilization, which are as much a part of God
as the rose or the earthquake, the shoal of fish or the work of art.
Nothing is outside God. I have sought to love in such a fashion
that love flowing out of me will spread as far as may be.

Petru Dmitriu, *Incognito*

PRAYERS

We pray for
   the spread of the Gospel
   missionary societies
   those who serve the Church at home and overseas
   those engaged in Christian publishing

Almighty God,
you show to those who are in error
   the light of your truth,
that they may return to the way of righteousness.
May we and all who have been admitted
   to the fellowship of Christ's religion
reject those things which are contrary to our profession
and follow all such things as are agreeable to the same;
through Jesus Christ our Lord.

Our Father

God our Saviour wants all men to be saved and to come to know
the truth.

Live as free men; do not use your freedom, however, to cover up any evil, but live as God's slaves.

1 Peter 2: 16

PSALM *Jubilate*

O shout to the Lord in triumph, all the earth:
serve the Lord with gladness, and come before his face with
  songs of joy.

Know that the Lord he is God:
it is he who has made us and we are his; we are his people
  and the sheep of his pasture.

Come into his gates with thanksgiving, and into his courts
  with praise:
give thanks to him, and bless his holy name.

For the Lord is good, his loving mercy is for ever:
his faithfulness throughout all generations.

Psalm 100 (99)

BIBLE READING

When you were slaves of sin, you were free from the control of righteousness; and what was the gain? Nothing but what now makes you ashamed, for the end of that is death. But now, freed from the commands of sin, and bound to the service of God, your gains are such as make for holiness, and the end is eternal life. For sin pays a wage, and the wage is death, but God gives freely, and his gift is eternal life, in union with Christ Jesus our Lord.

Romans 6: 20–3

For Paul, liberty is the basic datum which he respects, and struggles for, so that his communities may follow him not out of constraint and force, but freely. Of course, where there was a risk of abandonment of Christ and his gospel in favour of another gospel, he had to use the threat of anathema and excommunication. But what he did in regard to an individual (temporary excommunication in the hope of an improvement) he never practised in respect of a community, even in cases of major deviations. Paul was always very careful to avoid using his mandatory power. Instead of issuing prohibitions he appealed to individuals' judgment and responsibility. Instead of using constraint, he sought to convince. Instead of imposing himself, he exhorted. He said 'we . . . ', not 'you . . . '; he did not issue sanctions but used forgiveness; and ultimately did not stifle but stimulated freedom.

Hans Küng, *Why Priests?*

PRAYERS

We pray for
   those who witness to the Christian faith in difficult
      circumstances
   those who are prisoners for the sake of truth
   those who seek freedom from evil

Almighty God
you have broken the tyranny of sin
and have sent the Spirit of your Son into our hearts
whereby we call you Father
Give us grace to dedicate our freedom to your service
that all mankind may be brought
   to the glorious liberty of the sons of God;
through Jesus Christ our Lord.

Our Father

Live as free men; do not use your freedom, however, to cover up any evil, but live as God's slaves.

Second Week After Pentecost: Sunday

When anyone is joined to Christ, he is a new being.

2 Corinthians 5: 17

PSALM

Happy indeed is the man
who follows not the counsel of the wicked;
nor lingers in the way of sinners
nor sits in the company of scorners,
but whose delight is in the law of the Lord
and who ponders his law day and night.

He is like a tree that is planted
beside the flowing waters,
that yields its fruit in due season
and whose leaves shall never fade;
and all that he does shall prosper.

Psalm 1: 1–3

BIBLE READING

You must be made new in mind and spirit, and put on the new nature of God's creating, which shows itself in the just and devout life called for by the truth.

Then throw off falsehood; speak the truth to each other, for all of us are the parts of one body.

If you are angry, do not let anger lead you into sin; do not let sunset find you still nursing it; leave no loophole for the devil.

The thief must give up stealing, and instead work hard and honestly with his own hands, so that he may have something to share with the needy.

No bad language must pass your lips, but only what is good and helpful to the occasion, so that it brings a blessing to those who hear it. And do not grieve the Holy Spirit of God, for that Spirit is the seal with which you were marked for the day of our final liberation. Have done with spite and passion, all angry shouting and cursing, and bad feeling of every kind.

Be generous to one another, tender-hearted, forgiving one another as God in Christ forgave you.

Ephesians 4: 24–32

Resurrection as a present miracle . . . is to be found precisely within the ordinary round and daily routine of our lives. Resurrection occurs to us as we are, and its coming is generally quiet and unobtrusive and we may hardly be aware of its creative power. It is often only later that we realize that in some way or other we have been raised to newness of life, and so have heard the voice of the Eternal Word . . . A married couple find their old relationship, once rich and fulfilling, slowly drying up into no more than an external observance to the point where it seemed impossible that these dry bones should ever live again. Then a new relationship emerges, less superficially high-powered and less greedy than the old one, but deeper, more stable, more satisfying, with a new quality of life which is inexhaustible because it does not depend on the constant recharging of emotional batteries. That is resurrection.

H. A. Williams, *True Resurrection*

PRAYERS

We give thanks for
    our experiences of the risen life
    anything which has given us a new zest for life

We pray for those
    who find their lives monotonous and uninteresting
    who seek to bring new life to others

Stir up, O Lord,
the wills of your faithful people;
that richly bearing the fruit of good works,
they may by you be richly rewarded;
through Jesus Christ our Lord.

Our Father

When anyone is joined to Christ, he is a new being.

Second Week After Pentecost: Monday

Put on all the armour that God gives you, so that you will stand up against the Devil's evil tricks.

Ephesians 6: 11

PSALM

As for God, his ways are perfect;
the word of the Lord, purest gold.
He indeed is the shield
of all who make him their refuge.

For who is God but the Lord?
Who is a rock but our God?
The God who girds me with strength
and makes the path safe before me.

My feet you made swift as the deer's,
you have made me stand firm on the heights.
You have trained my hands for battle
and my arms to bend the heavy bow.

Psalm 18 (17): 31–5

BIBLE READING

In everything we do we show that we are God's servants, by enduring troubles, hardships, and difficulties with great patience. We have been beaten, jailed, and mobbed; we have been overworked and have gone without sleep or food. By our purity, knowledge, patience, and kindness we have shown ourselves to be God's servants; by the Holy Spirit, by our true love, by our message of truth, and by the power of God. We have righteousness as our weapon, both to attack and to defend ourselves. We are honoured and disgraced; we are insulted and praised. We are treated as liars, yet we speak the truth; as unknown, yet we are known by all; as though we were dead, but, as you see, we live on. Although punished, we are not killed; although saddened, we are always glad; we seem poor but we make many people rich; we seem to have nothing, yet we really possess everything.

2 Corinthians 6: 4–10

Then Apollyon espying his opportunity, began to gather up close to Christian, and wrestling with him, gave him a dreadful fall; and with that Christian's Sword flew out of his hand. Then said Apollyon, I am sure of thee now: and with that he had almost pressed him to death, so that Christian began to despair of life. But as God would have it, while Apollyon was fetching of his last blow, thereby to make a full end of this good man, Christian nimbly reached out his hand for his Sword, and caught it, saying, Rejoice not against me, O mine Enemy! When I call I shall arise; and with that gave him a deadly thrust, which made him give back, as one that had received his mortal wound: Christian perceiving that, made at him again, saying, Nay, in all these things we are more than conquerors through him that loved us. And with that Apollyon spread forth his Dragon's wings, and sped him away, that Christian for a season saw him no more.

John Bunyan, *The Pilgrim's Progress*

PRAYERS

We pray for
    those who are in danger, physical, mental or spiritual
    those who seek to cure mental or spiritual illness
    those who need help

Lord of all power and might,
you have called us to fight by your side
    against the tyranny of evil.
Arm us with the weapons of righteousness
that we may be equipped
    to repulse all assaults of the enemy
and to stand fast in the power of the Spirit;
through Jesus Christ our Lord.

Our Father

Put on all the armour that God gives you, so that you will stand up against the Devil's evil tricks.

Second Week After Pentecost: Tuesday

Father! May they be in us, just as you are in me and I am in you.

John 17: 21

HYMN *St Patrick's Breastplate*

Christ be with me, Christ within me,
Christ behind me, Christ before me,
Christ beside me, Christ to win me,
Christ to comfort and restore me.

Christ beneath me, Christ above me,
Christ in quiet, Christ in danger,
Christ in heart of all that love me,
Christ in mouth of friend and stranger.

BIBLE READING

Jesus spoke these words: 'I thank thee, Father, Lord of heaven and earth, for hiding these things from the learned and wise, and revealing them to the simple. Yes, Father, such was thy choice. Everything is entrusted to me by my Father; and no one knows the Son but the Father, and no one knows the Father but the Son and those to whom the Son may choose to reveal him.

Come to me, all whose work is hard, whose load is heavy; and I will give you relief. Bend your necks to my yoke, and learn from me, for I am gentle and humble-hearted; and your soul will find relief. For my yoke is good to bear, my load is light'.

Matthew 11: 25–30

The divine life is the pervading Presence of the Holy Spirit in everything . . . He is in us, welling up from the Father and dwelling in us, in the innermost recesses of our hearts, 'more intimate to us even than we are intimate to ourselves' (St Augustine), and making us inwardly present also to each other, in the same way as the Son and the Father really abide in each other. The Spirit is present in the whole creation, preparing for the final gathering up of all into Christ, the Son. He is present in the core of each being, in the heart of each man, as a ceaseless call and longing, as an unquenchable thirst for this unity and *koinonia*. In him the elect already possess and enjoy the *things-to-come*, for all things to come are already present in the eternity of God, and he who possesses the Spirit possesses everything that belongs to the Father and the Son.

Abhishikta Nanda, *Prayer*

PRAYERS

We pray for
    those who seek to know the mind of Christ
    religious communities
    clergy and lay workers
    theological colleges

Soul of Christ, sanctify me,
Body of Christ, save me.
Blood of Christ, refresh me.
Water from the side of Christ, wash me.
Passion of Christ, strengthen me.
O Good Jesus, hear me.
Within your wounds hide me.
Suffer me not to be separated from you.
From the malicious enemy defend me,
In the hour of my death call me and bid me come to you,
That with your saints I may praise you for ever and ever.

Our Father

Father! May they be in us, just as you are in me and I am in you.

Second Week After Pentecost: Wednesday

To have faith is to be sure of the things we hope for, to be certain of the things we cannot see.

Hebrews 11: 1

HYMN *Firmly I Believe*

Firmly I believe and truly
God is three and God is One;
And I next acknowledge duly
Manhood taken by the Son.

And I trust and hope most fully
In that Manhood crucified;
And each thought and deed unruly
Do to death, as he has died.

Simply to his grace and wholly
Light and life and strength belong,
And I love supremely, solely,
Him the Holy, him the Strong.

J. H. Newman

BIBLE READING

Now that we have been put right with God through faith, we have peace with God through our Lord Jesus Christ. He has brought us, by faith, into this experience of God's grace, in which we now live. We rejoice, then, in the hope we have of sharing God's glory! And we also rejoice in our troubles, because we know that trouble produces endurance, endurance brings God's approval, and his approval creates hope. This hope does not disappoint us, because God has poured out his love into our hearts by means of the Holy Spirit, who is God's gift to us.

Romans 5: 1–5

True faith is confident, and will venture all the world upon the strength of its persuasion. Will you lay your life on it, your estate and your reputation, that the doctrine of Jesus Christ is true in every article? Then you have true faith. But he that fears men more than God, believes men more than he believes in God.

Faith, if it be true, living, and justifying, cannot be separated from the good life; it works miracles, makes a drunkard become sober, a lascivious person become chaste, a covetous man become liberal; 'it overcomes the world – it work righteousness', and makes us diligently to do, and cheerfully to suffer, whatsoever God hath placed in our way to heaven.

Jeremy Taylor, *Holy Living*

PRAYERS

We give thanks for
the faithful witness of Christians throughout the ages

We pray
that the Church today may be faithful in its witness
for the gift of faith in times of difficulty and danger

Almighty and everliving God,
increase in us your gift of faith;
that, forsaking what lies behind
and reaching out to that which is before us,
we may run the way of your commandments
and win the crown of everlasting joy;
through Jesus Christ our Lord.

Our Father

To have faith is to be sure of the things we hope for, to be certain of the things we cannot see.

Second Week After Pentecost: Thursday

Let love make you serve one another.

Galatians 5: 13

HYMN *The Caring Church*

The Church of Christ, in every age
    Beset by change but Spirit led,
Must claim and test her heritage
    and keep on rising from the dead.

She has no mission but to serve,
    In proud obedience to her Lord;
To care for all, without reserve,
    To spread his liberating word.

Across a world, across the street,
    The victims of injustice cry
For shelter and for bread to eat,
    And never live before they die.

Then let the Servant Church arise,
    A caring Church that longs to be
A partner in Christ's sacrifice,
    And clothed in Christ's humanity.

F. Pratt Green

BIBLE READING

After he had washed his disciples' feet, Jesus put his outer garment
back on and returned to his place at the table. 'Do you understand what I have done to you?' he asked. 'You call me Teacher
and Lord, and it is right that you do so, because I am. I am your
Lord and Teacher, and I have just washed your feet. You, then,
should wash each other's feet. I have set an example for you. I
tell you the truth: no slave is greater than his master; no
messenger is greater than the one who sent him. Now you know
this truth; how happy you will be if you put it into practice!'

John 13: 12–17

The shining light in North India is Mother Teresa of Calcutta. I was fortunate enough to visit her sisters of charity in Patna. We could only feel deeply ashamed of our own feeble efforts besides the extraordinary drive of these young women, most of them highly educated girls from prosperous homes, for whom every unwanted child, every dying cripple, every outcast shines with the life of Christ. Their work cuts right across cultural barriers in an unflinching devotion to the Gospel. 'Anything you do for one of my brothers here, you do for me.' True beauty lies in action – in the way each child was given a toy, even if it was only a plastic bottle with something inside to make it rattle, or in the way every old person was given some work, however simple, so that perhaps for the first time, they discovered a sense of dignity in being useful. I am reminded too, of meeting an aged nun who had spent her life working in an orphanage in a town called Bettiah. Now too feeble to work, she could only watch others, but she assured me that she kept herself busy. 'These girls have fifty children to care for,' she said. 'They often have to shorten their prayers. I pray for them.'

David Jasper, *Christian Witness in North India.*

PRAYERS

We pray for
    all who are engaged in social services
    all who care for others
    doctors, nurses and nursing communities

Almighty Father,
whose son Jesus Christ has taught us
that what we do for the least of our brethren
    we do also for him:
give us the will to be servants of others
as he was the servant of all,
who gave up his life and died for us
but is alive and reigns with you and the Holy Spirit
one God, now and for ever.

Our Father

      Let love make you serve one another.

Our message is that God was making friends of all men through Christ.

2 Corinthians 5: 19

PSALM

Praise the Lord!
For it is good to sing praises to our God;
for he is gracious, and a song of praise is seemly.

The Lord builds up Jerusalem;
he gathers the outcasts of Israel.

He heals the brokenhearted,
and binds up their wounds.

He determines the number of the stars,
he gives to all of them their names.

Great is our Lord, and abundant in power;
his understanding is beyond measure.

The Lord lifts up the downtrodden,
he casts the wicked to the ground.

Psalm 147 (146): 1–6

BIBLE READING

'You are the salt of the earth. But if salt becomes tasteless, what can make it salty again? it is good for nothing, and can only be thrown out to be trampled underfoot by men.

'You are the light of the world. A city built on a hill top cannot be hidden. No one lights a lamp to put it under a tub; they put it on the lamp-stand where it shines for everyone in the house. In the same way your light must shine in the sight of men, so that, seeing your good works, they may give the praise to your Father in heaven'.

Matthew 5: 13–16

As soon as ever a man sets himself seriously to aim at the Christian character, the devil at once puts this thought into his mind – Am I not aiming at what is too high to be practicable? . . . I must not be so unworldly, if I am to help men in this sort of world. Now our Lord at once anticipates this kind of argument. He says at once, as it were, No, you are to help men by being unlike them . . . Thus our Lord at once proceeds to answer the question, How is a character such as the beatitudes describe, planted in such a world as this, to effect good? It is to purify by its own distinctive savour, it is to be conspicuous by its own splendid truth to its ideal, it is to arrest attention by its powerful contrast to the world about it . . . Salt is that which keeps things pure by its emphatic antagonistic savour. Light is that which burns distinctively in the darkness. 'A city that is set on a hill' is a marked object, arresting attention over a whole country side.

C. Gore, *The Sermon on the Mount*

PRAYERS

We pray for
   all Christian congregations
   our own parishes and congregations
   those engaged in specialized chaplaincy work

Almighty God,
who called your Church to witness
that you were in Christ reconciling men to yourself:
help us so to proclaim the good news of your love,
that all who hear it may be reconciled to you:
through him who died for us and rose again
and reigns with you and the Holy Spirit,
one God, now and for ever.

Our Father

Our message is that God was making friends of all men through Christ.

Second Week After Pentecost: Saturday

As the sufferings of Christ abound in us, so also through Christ we find abundant support.

2 Corinthians 1: 5

PSALM

In you, O Lord, I take refuge.
Let me never be put to shame.
In your justice, set me free,
hear me and speedily rescue me.

Be a rock of refuge for me,
a mighty stronghold to save me,
for you are my rock, my stronghold.
For your name's sake, lead me and guide me.

Release me from the snares they have hidden
for you are my refuge, Lord.
Into your hands I commend my spirit.
It is you who will redeem me, Lord.

Psalm 31 (30): 1–6

BIBLE READING

My dear friends, do not be surprised at the painful test you are suffering, as though something unusual were happening to you. Rather be glad that you are sharing Christ's sufferings, so that you may be full of joy when his glory is revealed. Happy are you if you are insulted because you are Christ's followers; this means that the glorious Spirit, the Spirit of God, is resting on you. None of you should suffer because he is a murderer, or a thief, or a criminal, or tries to manage other people's business. But if you suffer because you are a Christian, don't be shamed of it, but thank God that you bear Christ's name.

1 Peter 4: 12–16

I know a man who was blinded in the war . . . At first he bitterly resented what had happened to him. Then gradually he began to accept not only his blindness, but also his immense resentment at it. After about a year, he discovered that he could compose music . . . His music has not yet been published. Perhaps it never will be. But that is irrelevant. He wasn't looking for fame or reputation. He was looking for life. And he found it in the music he composes . . . This man had been with Jesus in Gethsemane . . . Jesus spoke of his passion and death, all the agony of it, as the cup He had to drink. He gives this cup to us to drink with Him. This means pain, and to drink the cup is to accept the pain. But then we find that the cup is something else as well, which is more important and final: the cup of blessing which is the communion of the blood of Christ.

H. A. Williams, *The True Wilderness*

PRAYERS

We pray for those who suffer
   through sickness and disease
   mentally and spiritually
   for the sake of truth

Lord God,
whose blessed Son our Saviour
gave his back to the smiters
and did not hide his face from shame:
give us grace to endure the sufferings of this present time
with sure confidence in the glory that shall be revealed;
through Jesus Christ our Lord.

Our Father

As the sufferings of Christ abound in us, so also through Christ
we find abundant support.

Third Week After Pentecost: Sunday

Love your neighbour as yourself.

Matthew 19: 19

HYMN *Incognito*

We find thee, Lord, in others' needs,
    we see thee in our brothers;
By loving word and kindly deed
    we serve the Man for Others.

We look around and see thy face
    disfigured, marred, neglected;
We find thee Lord in every place,
    sought for and unexpected.

We offer in simplicity
    our loving gift and labour;
And what we do, we do to thee,
    incarnate in our neighbour.

We love since we are loved by thee;
    new strength from thee we gather;
And in thy service we shall be
    made perfect with each other.

Giles Ambrose

BIBLE READING

Jesus said to the lawyer,

There was a man who was going down from Jerusalem to Jericho, when robbers attacked him, stripped him and beat him up, leaving him half dead. It so happened that a priest was going down that road; when he saw the man he walked on by, on the other side. In the same way a Levite also came there, went over and looked at the man, then walked on by, on the other side. But a certain Samaritan who was travelling that way came upon him, and when he saw the man his heart was filled with pity. He went over to him, poured oil and wine on his wounds and bandaged them; then he put the man on his own animal and took him to an inn, where he took care of him. The next day he took out two silver coins and gave them to the innkeeper. 'Take care of him', he told the innkeeper, 'and when I come back this way I will pay you back whatever you spend on him'.

Luke 10: 30–35

(The parable) means more than the obvious thing that the neighbour whom you are to love is anybody whom you may find in real need. It means that; but first of all love must be learnt by being loved. You cannot set out to do good, unless you first learn that of all the world you need more than anyone to have good done to you. The lawyer is bidden to see himself in the picture as the man by the roadside: naked, wounded, starving. He must learn that he must first be clothed, healed, housed, and fed. Then, not from a pedestal of superiority, but as one who has himself repented and suffered, and received all that he has that is worth having, he can go and do good to others ... The parable, indeed, contains the whole of St Paul's doctrine of salvation ... and it is summarised, as is indeed the whole of the Gospel of Christ, in 'Herein is love, not that we loved God, but that He loved us.'

F. C. N. Hicks, *The Fullness of Sacrifice*

PRAYERS

We pray for
  our friends and neighbours
  all whom we meet today
  all who listen to and help those in trouble
  the outcasts from society
  welfare organizations

God our Father
you have taught us through your Son
that love is the fulfilling of the law.
Grant to your servants that, loving one another,
they may continue in your love
  until their lives' end;
through Jesus Christ our Lord.

Our Father

Love your neighbour as yourself.

Third Week After Pentecost: Monday

Every family in heaven and on earth receives its true name from the Father.

Ephesians 3: 15

POEM *Home*

A home is a treasury of God
Where purity, beauty and joy
Are stored, for his purposes, inviolate.
For a home is in itself the triumph of God
Banishing Night, and Chaos and Necessity,
Indwelling this lifeless day
With the Spirit divine of freedom and joy.

R. Hoyland

BIBLE READING

A man who loves his wife loves himself . . . As the Scripture says, 'For this reason, a man will leave his father and mother, and unite with his wife, and the two will become one'. There is great truth revealed in this scripture, and I understand it applies to Christ and the church. But it also applies to you: every husband must love his wife as himself, and every wife must respect her husband.

Children, it is your Christian duty to obey your parents, for this is the right thing to do. 'Honour your father and mother' is the first commandment that has a promise added: 'so that all may be well with you, and you may live a long time in the land'. Parents, do not treat your children in such a way as to make them angry. Instead, raise them with Christian discipline and instruction.

Ephesians 5: 28–6: 4

Family happiness is always liable to founder on the hidden rocks and reefs of the unconscious life of its members. Christian acceptance of this involves the abandonment of all the extravagant expectations set up by the assumption that Christian family life ought to be a realm of frictionless loving. This in turn means that there will be less surprise and resentment and guilt when trouble comes and more chance of success in straightening things out. There is generally some straightening out to be done, human beings being what they are – creatures who do not as a rule do much harm except to those within range and most cruelly to those within closest range, brother, sister, parent, child, husband, wife. We all live hurt and hurting lives . . . But our lives are also the kind that are shaken periodically by beauty and other intensity of happiness, and again and again we are saved by love. This presence of love in family life is often unacknowledged, even unrecognized, because its nature is so much more akin to air we breathe than to thoughts we articulate.

J. Neville Ward, *Five for Sorrow, Ten for Joy*

PRAYERS

We pray for
    members of our family
    those whose homes are broken
    those without homes and the lonely
    orphans and those who care for them.

Lord God,
the protector of all who trust in you,
without whom nothing is strong, nothing is holy:
increase and multiply upon us your mercy,
that you being our ruler and guide,
we may so pass through things temporal
that we finally lose not the things eternal.
Grant this, heavenly Father,
for the sake of Jesus Christ our Lord.

Our Father

Every family in heaven and on earth receives its true name from the Father.

Third Week After Pentecost: Tuesday

There is no permanent city for us here on earth; we are looking for the city which is to come.

Hebrews 13: 14

PSALM

O pray for the peace of Jerusalem:
may those who love you prosper.

Peace be within your walls:
and prosperity in your palaces.

For the sake of my brothers and companions:
I will pray that 'peace be with you'.

For the sake of the house of the Lord our God:
I will seek for your good.

Psalm 122 (121): 6–9

BIBLE READING

I did not see a temple in the city, because its temple is the Lord God, the Almighty, and the Lamb. The city has no need of the sun or the moon to shine on it, because the glory of God shines in it, and the Lamb is its lamp. The peoples of the world will walk by its light, and the kings of the earth will bring their wealth into it. The gates of the city will stand open all day; they will never be closed, because there will be no night there. The greatness and the wealth of the nations will be brought into the city. But nothing that is impure will enter the city, nor anyone who does shameful things or tells lies.

Revelation 21: 22–7

One of Paul's great words is that which is variously translated 'communion' or 'fellowship'. The Greek word is *koinonia*, which was originally a commercial term implying co-partnership or common possession. Thus in the Gospels the sons of Zebedee and of John are said to have been *koinonia;* or partners in a kind of joint-stock company owning fishing-boats. This word seemed to the early Christians the most appropriate term to describe their relations one to another. They were co-partners in a great estate – the splendid spiritual 'heritage' in which they were 'joint-heirs with Christ'. The ground of their corporate life was what they called 'partnership of the Spirit' . . . Here as Paul saw, was in actual being that holy commonwealth of God for which the ages waited. Here was a community created not by geographical accident or by natural heredity, not based on conquest, or wealth, or government, but coming into existence by the spontaneous outburst of a common life in a multitude of persons. The free, joyous experience of the sons of God had created a family of God, inseparably one in Him: 'one person in Christ Jesus'.

C. H. Dodd, *The Meaning of Paul for Today*

PRAYERS

We pray
    that all men may live as good citizens
    for civic and local authorities
    for good relations between Church and State

Merciful God,
you have prepared for those who love you
such good things as pass man's understanding.
Pour into our hearts such love towards you
that we, loving you above all things,
may obtain your promises,
which exceed all that we can desire;
through Jesus Christ our Lord.

Our Father

There is no permanent city for us here on earth; we are looking for the city which is to come.

Third Week After Pentecost: Wednesday

The earth is the Lord's and all that is in it.

Psalm 24: 1

HYMN *God's Farm*

God, whose farm is all creation,
  take the gratitude we give;
Take the finest of our harvest,
  crops we grow that men may live.

Take our ploughing, seeding, reaping,
  hopes and fears of sun and rain,
All our thinking, planning, waiting,
  ripened in this fruit and grain.

All our labour, all our watching,
  all our calendar of care,
In these crops of your creation,
  take, O God: they are our prayer.

John Arlott

BIBLE READING

Remember this: the man who plants few seeds will have a small crop; the one who plants many seeds will have a large crop. Each one should give, then, as he has decided, not with regret or out of a sense of duty; for God loves the one who gives gladly. And God is able to give you more than you need, so that you will always have all you need for yourselves and more than enough for every good cause. As the scripture says,

He gives generously to the poor;
his kindness lasts forever.

And God, who supplies seed for the sower and bread to eat, will also supply you with all the seed you need and make it grow, to produce a rich harvest from your generosity. He will always make you rich enough to be generous at all times, so that many will thank God for your gifts.

2 Corinthians 9: 6–11

If bread and wine are in one sense the fruits of creation, they are not the sort that an animal could gather . . . Their material must be planted and reaped . . . He who has cleared a field and will keep it clean, attempts redemption; and he who plants, buries his own life with the seed; and he who waits upon the stars and seasons, recognizes a ruler of them . . . And in bettering his corn and his land, as in combating pests and the weather, he effectually becomes a scientist and clothes himself with creation . . . Yet even this does not give him bread or wine, but only grain and the grape . . . He must now make another interchange with creation . . . This time the interchange is with or through his fellows, so that the social life of man appears . . . As a consequence opportunities for division of labour and trade appear, and further opportunities for combination and exchange, and for trust between men. The bread itself could create a social pattern and also become a symbol of it.

Fr. Hugh S.S.F., The Burning Glass

PRAYERS

We thank God for all the blessings of the harvest

We pray for
   those who work on the land or at sea
   seasonable weather
   those who have insufficient food

Almighty God,
whose will it is that the earth
should bear its fruits in their seasons:
direct the labours of those who work on the land,
that they may employ the resources of nature
   for our own well-being
and the relief of those in need:
through Jesus Christ our Lord.

Our Father

   The earth is the Lord's and all that is in it.

We must always aim at those things that bring peace, and that help to strengthen one another.

Romans 14: 19

POEM *From* 'The Rock'

In the vacant places
We will build with new bricks
There are hands and machines
And clay for new brick
And lime for new mortar
Where the bricks are fallen
We will build with new stone
Where the beams are rotten
We will build with new timbers
Where the word is unspoken
We will build with new speech
There is work together
A Church for all
And a job for each
Every man to his work.

T. S. Eliot

BIBLE READING

Whoever does not agree with the true words of our Lord Jesus Christ and with the teachings of our religion is swollen with pride and knows nothing. He has an unhealthy desire to argue and quarrel about words, and this brings on jealousy, dissension, insults, evil suspicions, and constant arguments from men whose minds do not function and who no longer have the truth. They think that religion is a way to become rich.

Well, religion does make a man very rich, if he is satisfied with what he has. What did we bring into the world? Nothing! What can we take out of the world? Nothing! . . . But those who want to get rich fall into temptation and are caught in the trap of many foolish and harmful desires, which pull men down to ruin and destruction. For the love of money is a source of all kinds of evil. Some have been so eager to have it that they have wandered away from the faith and have broken their hearts with many sorrows.

1 Timothy 6: 3–7. 9–10

In practice, industrial life has to proceed by consultation and negotiation, by debate and bargain, over the detail of daily industrial affairs and industry's inevitable conflicts. This needs skilled professional men of integrity and intelligence, if it is to make for the benefit of industry, and of the society it serves. The extent to which this succeeds depends not least on the general atmosphere of trust between groups and individuals in which the detailed procedure takes place. If Christians are looking for areas in industry where individuals can commit themselves widely and deeply to working for love, at cost, in faith and hope, this is it. A vast amount of important and wide-ranging industrial activity depends for its success on the costly and persistent efforts of individuals in all levels to work for trust and to sustain it, come what may.

Simon Phipps, *God on Monday*

PRAYERS

We pray for
   those engaged in commerce and industry
   good relations between employer and employed
   those who work in industrial chaplaincies
   those whose work is hazardous or dangerous
   the unemployed

Almighty God,
you have provided the resources of the world
to maintain the life of your children,
and have so ordered our life
that we are dependent upon each other.
Bless all men in their daily work,
and, as you have given us the knowledge to produce plenty,
so give us the will to bring it within the reach of all;
through Jesus Christ our Lord.

Our Father

We must always aim at those things that bring peace, and that help to strengthen one another.

Third Week After Pentecost: Friday

I am among you as one who serves.

Luke 22: 27

PSALM

O Lord, my heart is not proud
nor haughty my eyes.
I have not gone after things too great
nor marvels beyond me.

Truly I have set my soul
in silence and peace.
A weaned child on its mother's breast,
even so is my soul.

O Israel, hope in the Lord
both now and for ever.

Psalm 131 (130)

BIBLE READING

When Jesus entered Capernaum, a Roman officer met him and begged for help: 'Sir, my servant is at home, sick in bed, unable to move and suffering terribly'. 'I will go and make him well,' Jesus said. 'Oh no, sir,' answered the officer. 'I do not deserve to have you come into my house. Just give the order and my servant will get well. I, too, am a man under the authority of superior officers, and I have soldiers under me. I order this one, "Go!" and he goes; and I order that one, "Come!" and he comes; and I order my slave, "Do this!" and he does it.' Jesus was surprised when he heard this, and said to the people who were following him. 'I tell you. I have never seen such faith as this in anyone in Israel' . . . And Jesus said to the officer, 'Go home, and what you believe will be done for you'.

Matthew 8: 5–10. 13

For let nobody be under any delusion; there is judgment in store, even for the hosts of heaven, the very angels in glory, the visible and invisible powers themselves, if they have no faith in the blood of Christ. Let him who can, absorb this truth. High position is no excuse for pride; it is faith and love that are everything, and these must come before all else. But look at the men who have those perverted notions about the grace of Jesus Christ which has come down to us, and see how contrary to the mind of Christ they are. They have no care for love, no thought for the widow and orphan, and none at all for the afflicted, the captive, the hungry or the thirsty.

Ignatius of Antioch, *To the Smyrnaeans* 6

PRAYERS

We pray for all
   who bear authority in government
   who teach and train others
   employers of labour
   parents and guardians

Father of mankind,
you gave your only-begotten Son
to take upon himself the form of a servant
and to be obedient even to death on a cross:
give us the same mind that was in Christ Jesus
that, sharing his humility,
we may come to be with him in his glory;
who is alive and reigns with you and the Holy Spirit,
one God, now and for ever.

I am among you as one who serves.

Not everyone who calls me 'Lord, Lord,' will enter into the kingdom of heaven, but only those who do what my Father in heaven wants them to do.

Matthew 7: 21

PSALM

This I know, that God is on my side.
In God, whose word I praise,
in the Lord, whose word I praise,
in God, I trust; I shall not fear:
what can mortal man do to me?

I am bound by the vows I have made you.
O God, I will offer you praise
for you rescued my soul from death,
you kept my feet from stumbling
that I may walk in the presence of God
in the light of the living.

Psalm 56 (55): 10–14

BIBLE READING

Jesus said, 'Everyone who hears these words of mine and obeys them will be like a wise man who built his house on the rock. The rain poured down, the rivers flooded over, and the winds blew hard against that house. But it did not fall, because it had been built on the rock.

But everyone who hears these words of mine and does not obey them will be like a foolish man who built his house on the sand. The rain poured down, the rivers flooded over, the winds blew hard against that house, and it fell. What a terrible fall that was!'

Matthew 7: 24–7

Many Christians (in Russia) believe that the promise to the apostolic community 'The gates of hell shall not prevail against it' was not an empty one. They, therefore, have deep theological reasons for supposing the Church will survive all the onslaughts of unbelievers. As for the Jewish faithful, they rest the survival and destiny of their community in the loving succour of the God of Abraham, Isaac and Jacob. Such matters are rooted in faith, which in the nature of things cannot be confirmed in advance of unfolding life experience, and they offer no acceptable guide to the future of any local religious community for those who confine themselves to external evidence. But there can be no disputing that many millions of religious believers in the Soviet Union today are sustained by their belief in the ultimate indestructibility of the community of faith and, by their deep devotion and heroic courage, they are turning this belief into reality.

Trevor Beeson, *Discretion and Valour*

PRAYERS

We give thanks for those who witness to the Christian faith.

We pray for
    Christians living in non-Christian countries
    Christians living in alien conditions
    the gift of faith

Lord of all power and might,
the author and giver of all good things:
graft in our hearts the love of your Name,
increase in us true religion,
nourish in us all goodness,
and of your great mercy keep us in the same;
through Jesus Christ our Lord.

Our Father

Not everyone who calls me 'Lord, Lord,' will enter into the kingdom of heaven, but only those who do what my Father in heaven wants them to do.

Fourth Week After Pentecost: Sunday

God saw all that he had made, and it was very good.

Genesis 1: 31

PSALM

How great is your name, O Lord our God,
through all the earth!

When I see the heavens, the work of your hands,
the moon and the stars which you have arranged,
what is man that you should keep him in mind,
mortal man that you care for him?

Yet you have made him little less than a God;
with glory and honour you crowned him,
gave him power over the works of your hand,
put all things under his feet.

Psalm 8: 1. 4–7

BIBLE READING

God said, 'Let us make man in our image and likeness to rule the fish in the sea, the birds of heaven, the cattle, all wild animals on earth, and all the reptiles that crawl upon the earth'. So God created man in his own image; in the image of God he created him; male and female he created them. God blessed them and said to them, 'Be fruitful and increase; fill the earth and subdue it, rule over the fish in the sea, the birds of heaven, and every living thing that moves upon the earth'. God also said, 'I give you all plants that bear seed everywhere on earth, and every tree bearing fruit which yields seed; they shall be yours for food. All green plants I give for food to the wild animals, to all the birds of heaven, and to all reptiles on earth, every living creature'.

Genesis 1: 26–30

When God planted a garden He set a man over it, and set the man under Himself. When He planted the garden of our nature and caused the flowering, fruiting trees to grow there, He set our will to 'dress' them. Compared with them it is dry and cold. And unless His grace comes down, like the rain and the sunshine, we shall use this tool to little purpose. But its laborious – and largely negative – services are indispensable. If they were needed when the Garden was still Paradise, how much more now when the soil has gone sour and the worst weeds seem to thrive on it best? But heaven forbid we should work in the spirit of prigs and Stoics. While we hack and prune we know very well that what we are hacking and pruning is big with a splendour and vitality which our rational will could never of itself have supplied. To liberate that splendour, to let it become fully what it is trying to be, to have tall trees instead of scrubby tangles, and sweet apples instead of crabs, is part of our purpose.

C. S. Lewis, *The Four Loves*

PRAYERS

We pray for
   all engaged in creative work, intellectual or practical
   employers of labour
   the Trade Unions

Almighty God,
you have created the heavens and the earth
and made man in your own image:
teach us to discern your hand in all your works
and to serve you with reverence and thanksgiving;
through Jesus Christ our Lord,
who with you and the Holy Spirit reigns supreme over all things
now and for ever. Amen.

Our Father

God saw all that he had made, and it was very good.

By myself I can serve God's law only with my mind, while my human nature serves the law of sin.

Romans 7: 25

PSALM

Out of the depths have I called to you, O Lord:
Lord, hear my voice;

O let your ears consider well:
the voice of my supplication.

If you, Lord, should note what we do wrong:
who then, O Lord, could stand?

But there is forgiveness with you:
so that you shall be feared.

I wait for the Lord; my soul waits for him:
and in his word is my hope.

He will redeem Israel:
from the multitude of his sins.

Psalm 130 (129): 1–5. 8

BIBLE READING

The death Christ died was death to sin, once and for all; and the life he now lives is life to God. In the same way you are to think of yourselves as dead to sin but alive to God in union with Christ Jesus. Sin must no longer rule in your mortal bodies, so that you obey the desires of your natural self. Nor must you surrender any part of yourselves to sin, to be used for wicked purposes. Instead, give yourselves to God, as men who have been brought from death to life, and surrender your whole being to him to be used for righteous purposes. Sin must not rule over you; you do not live under law but under God's grace.

Romans 6: 10–14

Edwin Muir had seen terrible suffering in man and beast, he had encountered poverty and anxiety and despair as the dominant characteristics of the social situation in which he lived. He saw the advance of tyranny in society, the eclipse of freedom, the iron grip of terror. Could the succession of historical events which he had watched and in which in no small measure he had participated, find any meaning within the total sweep of human history? Was there any meaningful centre of history to which his own sector of history could be related? I suggest that the key-phrase for the understanding of his poetic testimony is to be found in the words:

Did a God indeed in dying cross my life that day?

There is a cross-roads in history and there the paths of men and nations find their meaning and their goal.

F. W. Dillistone, *The Christian Understanding of Atonement*

PRAYERS

We pray for
  those overwhelmed by a sense of sin and guilt
  those who can see no difference between right and wrong
  the drop-outs from society
  those engaged in rescue work

Almighty God,
you have given your Son, Jesus Christ,
to break the power of evil.
Free us from all that darkens and ensnares us
and bring us to eternal light and joy;
through the power of him
who is alive and reigns with you and the Holy Spirit,
one God, now and for ever.

Our Father

By myself I can serve God's law only with my mind, while my human nature serves the law of sin.

God himself called you to share in the life of his Son Jesus Christ our Lord, and God keeps faith.

1 Corinthians 1: 9

PSALM

I remember the deeds of the Lord,
I remember your wonders of old,
I muse on all your works
and ponder your mighty deeds.

Your ways, O God, are holy.
What God is great as our God?
You are the God who works wonders.
You showed your power among the peoples.
Your strong arm redeemed your people,
the sons of Jacob and Joseph.

Psalm 77 (76): 12–16

BIBLE READING

The days are coming – it is God who speaks – when I will make a new covenant with the House of Israel and the House of Judah . . . Deep within them I will plant my Law, writing it on their hearts. Then I will be their God and they shall be my people. There will be no further need for neighbour to try to teach neighbour, or brother to say to brother, 'Learn to know God!' No, they shall all know me, the least no less than the greatest, since I will forgive their iniquity and never call their sin to mind.

Jeremiah 31: 31. 33–4

The covenant was Israel's acceptance of the overlordship of Jehovah . . . It was in no sense a bargain between equals, but a vassal's acceptance of the Overlord's terms. It therefore laid conditions on election and injected into Israel's notion of herself as a chosen people a moral note, which she would never be allowed to forget, try though she might. She was no superior people, favoured because she deserved it, but a helpless people who had been the recipient of unmerited grace. Her God-King was no national genius, bound to her by ties of blood and cult, but a cosmic God who had chosen her in her dire need, and whom she in a free moral act had chosen. Her society was thus grounded not in nature but in covenant.

John Bright, *A History of Israel*

PRAYERS

We pray for
   young nations
   young churches
   racial harmony
   the end of apartheid

Almighty God,
who alone can bring order
to the unruly wills and passions of sinful men
give us grace
   to love what you command
   and to desire what you promise
that in all the changes and chances of this world,
our hearts may surely there be fixed
where lasting joys are to be found;
through Jesus Christ our Lord.

Our Father

God himself called you to share in the life of his Son Jesus Christ our Lord; and God keeps faith.

He has sent me to proclaim release to the captives.

Luke 4: 18

PSALM

When the Lord turned the tide of Zion's fortune,
we were like men who had found new health.
Our mouths were full of laughter
and our tongues sang aloud for joy.
Then word went round among the nations,
'The Lord has done great things for them.'
Great things indeed the Lord then did for us,
and we rejoice.

Turn once again our fortune, Lord,
as streams return in the dry south.
Those who sow in tears
shall reap with songs of joy.

Psalm 126 (125): 1–5

BIBLE READING

The Lord said to Moses, 'Stretch out your hand over the sea, and let the water flow back over the Egyptians, their chariots and their cavalry.' So Moses stretched his hand over the sea, and at daybreak the water returned to its accustomed place; but the Egyptians were in flight as it advanced, and the Lord swept them out into the sea. The water flowed back and covered all Pharoah's army, the chariots and the cavalry, which had pressed the pursuit into the sea. Not one man was left alive. Meanwhile the Israelites had passed along the dry ground through the sea, with the water making a wall for them to right and to left.

Exodus 14: 26–9

When Pharaoh, that most savage and cruel tyrant, afflicted the free and noble people of the Hebrews, God sent Moses to lead them out of their debasing slavery at the hands of the Egyptians. Their doorposts were smeared with the blood of a lamb so that the destroyer might avoid the houses bearing the bloodstain, and thus against all expectation the Hebrews gained their freedom. But when they had been liberated they were pursued by the enemy, who saw the sea miraculously part to afford the Hebrews a path. Yet even so the Egyptians pressed on in their footsteps, and at once they were submerged and drowned in the Red Sea.

Now turn your mind from past to present, from symbol to reality. Of old Moses was sent into Egypt by God, but in our era Christ is sent into the world by the Father. As Moses was appointed to lead his afflicted people from Egypt, so Christ came to deliver the people of the world who were overcome by sin.

Cyril of Jerusalem, *Mystagogic Catechesis* 1, 2–3

PRAYERS

We pray for
    those addicted to alcohol and drugs
    victims of oppression and persecution
    the exploited
    social workers

Lord God our redeemer,
who heard the cry of your people
and sent your servant Moses to lead them out of slavery;
free us from the tyranny of sin and death
and, by the leading of your Spirit,
bring us to our promised land;
through Jesus Christ our Lord.

Our Father

    He has sent me to proclaim release to the captives.

Fourth Week After Pentecost: Thursday

Whoever wants to serve me must follow me, so that my servant will be with me where I am.

John 12: 26

PSALM

They are happy whose life is blameless,
who follow God's law!
They are happy those who do his will,
seeking him with all their hearts,
who never do anything evil
but walk in his ways.
You have laid down your precepts
to be obeyed with care.
May my footsteps be firm
to obey your statutes.
Then I shall not be put to shame
as I heed your commands.

Psalm 119 (118): 1-6

BIBLE READING

As Jesus walked by Lake Galilee, he saw two fishermen, Simon and his brother Andrew, catching fish in the lake with a net. Jesus said to them, 'Come with me and I will teach you to catch men'. At once they left their nets and went with him. He went a little farther on and saw two other brothers, James and John the sons of Zebedee. They were in their boats getting their nets ready. As soon as Jesus saw them he called them; they left their father Zebedee in the boat with the hired men and went with Jesus.

Mark 1: 16–20

Remember the axiom that 'the good is always the enemy of the better'. Men cling to the lower blessings which they know, and shrink from the higher which they do not know and therefore fear. Comfort is good, education is good and many rest in them. Yet both are or may be purely selfish. But the things of the Spirit, which are wholly unselfish and have no market value, and rest upon communion with God in Christ who can only be known by the way of the Cross – these have few lovers. If your deliberate aim in life is the establishment within you and without you of the Kingdom of Christ and of God, then all your schemes and projects, whatever they are, will be aimed at as elements in that Kingdom. After all, the greatest reformers the world has ever known were the eleven men who were true to Christ.

H. F. B. Mackay, *Difficulties in the Way of Discipleship*

PRAYERS

We pray for
the unity of all Christian people
all Church leaders
the local Church
the children of the Church

Almighty God,
by whose grace alone we are accepted
and called to your service:
strengthen us by your Holy Spirit
and make us worthy of our calling;
through Jesus Christ our Lord.

Our Father

Whoever wants to serve me must follow me, so that my servant will be with me where I am.

Fourth Week After Pentecost: Friday

May your kingdom come.

Matthew 6: 10

PSALM

He is happy who is helped by Jacob's God,
whose hope is in the Lord his God.
It is he who keeps faith for ever,
who is just to those who are oppressed.
It is he who gives bread to the hungry,
the Lord, who sets prisoners free,

The Lord, who gives sight to the blind,
who raises up those who are bowed down,
the Lord, who protects the stranger
and upholds the widow and orphan.

The Lord will reign for ever,
Sion's God, from age to age.

Psalm 146 (145): 5–10

BIBLE READING

Jesus unrolled the scroll and found the place where it is written,
'The Spirit of the Lord is upon me, because he has chosen me to
preach the Good News to the poor. He has sent me to proclaim
liberty to the captives, and recovery of sight to the blind; to set
free the oppressed, and announce the year when the Lord will
save his people.' Jesus rolled up the scroll, gave it back to the
attendant and sat down. All the people in the synagogue had
their eyes fixed on him. He began speaking to them, 'This passage
of scripture has come true today, as you heard it being read'.

Luke 4: 17–21

The ultimate hope of the believer is directed towards the Kingdom of God, beyond death and beyond the structures of the world. This ultimate hope is nourished by his belief that God has raised Jesus from the dead into his Kingdom beyond death. At the same time his penultimate hope is for a 'better world' here and now, that is, for a world in which the creative and the redemptive love of God is more fully realized. This penultimate hope is nourished both by his ultimate hope and also by those features of his secular experience which support and encourage an affirmative attitude towards the future, and which he reads as signs of the providence of God in nature, history and the lives of individual men and women.

Peter Baelz, *The Forgotten Dream*

PRAYERS

We pray for
    those who work for the spread of the Gospel
    the lay ministries of the Church
    those who work in the social services
    doctors, nurses and medical students

Almighty God,
you have made us for yourself
and our souls are restless
till they find their rest in you.
Teach us to offer ourselves to your service,
that here we may have your peace,
and in the world to come may see you face to face;
through Jesus Christ our Lord.

Our Father

May your Kingdom come.

Fourth Week After Pentecost: Saturday

We all, with unveiled face, beholding the glory of the Lord, are being changed into his likeness from one degree of glory to another.

2 Corinthians 3: 18

HYMN

More bright than day thy face did show,
Thy raiment whiter than the snow,
When on the mount to mortals blest
Man's Maker thou was manifest.

May all who seek thy praise aright
Through purer lives show forth thy light;
So to the brightness of the skies
By holy deeds our hearts shall rise.

10th century office hymn

BIBLE READING

We have not depended on made-up legends in making known to you the mighty coming of our Lord Jesus Christ. With our own eyes we saw his greatness. We were there when he was given honour and glory by God the Father, when the voice came to him from the Supreme Glory, saying, 'This is my own dear Son, with whom I am well pleased!' We ourselves heard this voice coming from heaven, when we were with him on the sacred mountain. So we are even more confident of the message proclaimed by the prophets. You will do well to pay attention to it because it is like a lamp shining in a dark place, until the Day dawns and the light of the morning star shines in your hearts.

2 Peter 1: 16–19

Peter on Mount Hermon may have longed to *return* to the happiness of his discipleship before the Passion was announced, or to *escape* from the conflict into a heavenly rest, or to *advance* at once into the peace of the last things. But the Transfiguration meant the taking of the whole conflict of the Lord's mission, just as it was, into the glory which gave meaning to it all. Confronted as he is with a universe more than ever terrible in the blindness of its processes and the destructiveness of its potentialities mankind must be led to the Christian faith not as a panacea of progress nor as an other-worldly solution unrelated to history, but as a Gospel of Transfiguration. He who is transfigured is the Son of Man; and, as He discloses on Mount Hermon another world, He reveals that no part of created things and no moment of created time lies outside the power of the Spirit, who is Lord, to change from glory into glory.

A. M. Ramsey, *The Glory of God and the Transfiguration of Christ*

PRAYERS

We pray
for grace to accept suffering and difficulty
for grace to recognize God at work in men's lives
for courage and hope to face the future
for Christians facing persecution

Almighty Father,
whose Son was revealed in majesty
before he suffered death upon the cross:
give us faith to perceive his glory,
that we may be strengthened to suffer with him
and be changed into his likeness,
from glory to glory;
who is alive and reigns with you and the Holy Spirit,
one God, now and for ever. Amen.

Our Father

We all, with unveiled face, beholding the glory of the Lord, are being changed into his likeness from one degree of glory to another.

Blessed Virgin Mary

Behold, I am the handmaid of the Lord; let it be to me according to your word.

Luke 1: 38

CANTICLE *The Magnificat*

My soul proclaims the greatness of the Lord,
my spirit rejoices in God my saviour;
for he has looked with favour on his lowly servant.
From this day all generations will call me blessed:
The Almighty has done great things for me,
and holy is his Name.

He has mercy on those who fear him
in every generation.
He has shown the strength of his arm,
he has scattered the proud in their conceit.
He has cast down the mighty from their thrones,
and has lifted up the lowly.
He has filled the hungry with good things,
and the rich he has sent away empty.

He has come to the help of his servant Israel
for he has remembered his promise of mercy,
the promise he has made to our fathers,
to Abraham and his children for ever.

BIBLE READING

In those days Mary arose and went with haste into the hill country, to a city of Judah, and she entered the house of Zechariah and greeted Elizabeth. And when Elizabeth heard the greeting of Mary, the babe leaped in her womb; and Elizabeth was filled with the Holy Spirit and she exclaimed with a loud cry, 'Blessed are you among women, and blessed is the fruit of your womb! And why is this granted me, that the mother of my Lord should come to me? For behold, when the voice of your greeting came to my ears, the babe in my womb leaped for joy. And blessed is she who believed that there would be a fulfilment of what was spoken to her from the Lord'.

Luke 1: 39–45

SECOND READING

Mary sang of her joy in God her Saviour, who shows mercy to all men on condition that they are willing to become poor and needy since then alone can they receive the certainty of being filled by Him. It is this love which, coming from the Lord, extends from age to age, from Abraham who left all to follow the search for God; it is this love which is extended through the poor of Israel, passing through Mary, the poor and blessed handmaid, and finding its fulfilment in Christ who had no place to lay his head and who for the rich became poor in order that he might enrich us by his poverty; it is this love which is extended through the Church of the poor in order to reach its fulfilment in the Kingdom of God, which belongs to the poor, the meek, the aflicted, the needy, and to those who show mercy, to the pure, to the peaceful and to the persecuted. Thus Mary believed and sang; and thus the Church believes and sings.

> Max Thurian, *Mary Mother of the Lord, the Figure of the Church*

PRAYERS

O my God, I am not mine own, but thine:
Take me and make me in all things to do thy most holy will.
O my God, I give myself to thee,
for joy or for sorrow, in sickness and in health,
for life and for death, for time and for eternity;
for Jesus Christ's sake, Amen.

Heavenly Father,
who chose the Virgin Mary, full of grace,
to be the mother of our Lord and Saviour:
fill us with your grace,
that in all things we may accept your holy will
and with her rejoice in your salvation;
through Jesus Christ our Lord.

Our Father

Behold, I am the handmaid of the Lord; let it be to me according to your word.

St Michael and All Angels

All the angels stood round the throne and they fell down on their faces and worshipped God.

Revelation 7: 11

PSALM

For you, the Lord is a safe retreat;
you have made the Most High your refuge.

No disaster shall befall you,
no calamity shall come upon your home.

For he has charged his angels
to guard you wherever you go,
to lift you on their hands
for fear you should strike your foot against a stone.

Psalm 91 (90): 9–12

BIBLE READING

The mind of the king of Syria was greatly troubled and he called his servants and said to them, 'Will you not show me who of us is for the king of Israel?' And one of his servants said, 'None, my lord, O king; but Elisha, the prophet who is in Israel, tells the king of Israel the words that you speak in your bedchamber'. And he said, 'Go and see where he is, that I may send and seize him'. It was told him, 'Behold, he is in Dothan'. So he sent there horses and chariots and a great army; and they came by night, and surrounded the city. And the servant of the man of God said, 'Alas, my master! What shall we do?' He said, 'Fear not, for those who are with us are more than those who are with them'. Then Elisha prayed, and said, 'O Lord, I pray thee, open his eyes that he may see'. So the Lord opened the eyes of the young man, and he saw; and behold, the mountain was full of horses and chariots of fire round about Elisha.

2 Kings 6: 11–17

Scripture refers to the direct ministry of angels much that we attribute to the 'laws of nature'. The wind, the cloud, the fire, the pestilence, the stroke of death, perhaps the very virtue of healing waters, are assigned to the action of personal beings, whose presence has been openly shown from time to time to assure our faith . . . Scripture tells us that messengers of God are about us on every side. The ministry of angels is the perfected type of our work. Are they the messengers of God? So are we, charged to declare one to another the truth we know. Are they the sons of God? So are we, by the power which Christ has given us. Are they called the 'watchers'? Such is the charge which the Lord has laid upon us. Are they called the 'holy ones'? Such is the character which we are commended to secure. Do they fulfil the will of God faithfully, cheerfully, perfectly? Day by day we pray that we may do that will on earth as they do it in heaven.

B. F. Westcott, *Village Sermons*

PRAYERS

With angels and archangels, and with all the company of heaven, we proclaim your great and glorious Name, for ever praising you and saying:
Holy, holy, holy Lord,
God of power and might,
heaven and earth are full of your glory.
    Hosanna in the highest.

Eternal Lord God,
you have appointed both angels and men
to worship and serve you in your kingdom.
As your holy angels stand before you in heaven,
so may they help and defend us here on earth;
through Jesus Christ our Lord.

Our Father

All the angels stood round the throne and they fell down on their faces and worshipped God.

Apostles

It is not ourselves that we preach: we preach Jesus Christ as Lord, and ourselves as your servants for Jesus' sake.

2 Corinthians 4: 5

HYMN *The eternal gifts of Christ the King*

The eternal gifts of Christ the King,
The apostles' glory, let us sing;
And all, with hearts of gladness, raise
Due hymns of thankful love and praise.

Theirs is the steadfast faith of saints,
And hope that never yields nor faints,
And love of Christ in perfect glow
That lays the prince of this world low.

To thee, Redeemer, now we cry,
That thou wouldst join to them on high
Thy servants, who this grace implore,
For ever and for evermore.

St Ambrose

BIBLE READING

The scripture says, 'Whoever believes in Jesus will not be disappointed.' This includes everyone, because there is no difference between Jews and Gentiles; God is the same Lord of all, and richly blesses all who call to him. As the scripture says, 'Everyone who calls on the name of the Lord will be saved.'

But how can they call to him, if they have not believed? And how can they believe, if they have not heard the message? And how can they hear, if the message is not proclaimed? And how can the message be proclaimed, if the messengers are not sent out? As the scripture says, 'How wonderful is the coming of those who bring good news!'

Romans 10: 11–15.

Scholars who like Nicodemus were quick to ask 'How can these things be?' were not of the right order for setting a great movement afoot. If men were fully possessed with the momentous nature of God's spiritual working in the world, the idea of this as a *fact* would take up all their minds leaving no room for the question of *mode*. If Nicodemus had been capable of seeing how sublime was the future presented to him, he would never have accepted *how* it could come to pass . . . Our Lord required men plastic and receptive, capable of devoted self-surrender and possessed of self-transforming and expanding powers . . . The minds of the Apostles were quite limpid; they received all 'as little children', registering truly what came from without, and declaring it just as their five senses set it before them.

H. Latham, *Pastor Pastorum*

PRAYERS

We thank God for the lives and work of the Apostles
especially . . .

We pray
that we may follow their example in proclaiming the faith
for all leaders of the Church

Almighty God,
you have built your Church
upon the foundation of the apostles and prophets
with Jesus Christ himself as the chief corner-stone.
So join us together in unity of spirit by their doctrine
that we may be made a holy temple acceptable to you;
through Jesus Christ our Lord.

Our Father

It is not ourselves that we preach: we preach Jesus Christ as Lord,
and ourselves as your servants for Jesus' sake.

Martyrs

How blest are those who have suffered persecution for the cause of right; the kingdom of Heaven is theirs.

Matthew 5: 10

PSALM

I love you, Lord, my strength,
my rock, my fortress, my saviour.
My God is the rock where I take refuge;
my shield, my mighty help, my stronghold.
The Lord is worthy of all praise:
when I call I am saved from my foes.

They assailed me in the day of my misfortune,
but the Lord was my support.
He brought me forth into freedom,
he saved me because he loved me.

Psalm 18 (17): 2-4. 19-20

BIBLE READING

Who, then, can separate us from the love of Christ? Can trouble do it, or hardship, or persecution, or hunger, or poverty, or danger, or death? As the scripture says, 'For your sake we are in danger of death the whole day long: we are treated like sheep that are going to be slaughtered.' No, in all these things we have complete victory through him who loved us! For I am certain that nothing can separate us from his love: neither death nor life; neither angels nor other heavenly rulers or powers; neither the present nor the future; neither the world above nor the world below – there is nothing in all creation that will ever be able to separate us from the love of God which is ours through Christ Jesus our Lord.

Romans 8: 35-9

We do not think of a martyr simply as a good Christian who has been killed because he is a Christian: for that would be solely to mourn. We do not think of him simply as a good Christian who has been elevated to the company of the Saints: for that would be simply to rejoice: and neither our mourning nor our rejoicing is as the world is. A Christian martyrdom is no accident. Saints are not made by accident. Still less is a Christian martyrdom the effect of a man's will to become a Saint, as a man by willing and contriving may become a ruler of men . . . A martyrdom is never the design of man; for the true martyr is he who has become the instrument of God, who has lost his will in the will of God, not lost it but found it, for he has found freedom in submission to God. The martyr no longer desires anything for himself, not even in the glory of martyrdom.

T. S. Eliot, Murder in the Cathedral

PRAYERS

We give thanks for all who have given their lives for Christ,
    especially . . .

We pray for those who persecute others

Almighty God,
by whose grace and power your holy martyr N
triumphed over suffering and was faithful unto death:
strengthen us with your grace,
that we may endure reproach and persecution
and faithfully bear witness to the Name of Jesus Christ our
    Lord;
who is alive and reigns with you and the Holy Spirit,
one God, now and for ever.

Our Father

How blest are those who have suffered persecution for the cause of right: the kingdom of Heaven is theirs.

Doctors and Confessors

Proclaim the message, press it home on all occasions, convenient or inconvenient, use argument, reproof, and appeal, with all the patience that the work of teaching requires.

2 Timothy 4: 2

PSALM

Do not take the word of truth from my mouth
for I trust in your decrees.
I shall always keep your law
for ever and ever.
I shall walk in the path of freedom
for I seek your precepts.
I will speak of your will before kings
and not be abashed.
Your commands have been my delight;
these I have loved.
I will worship your commands and love them
and ponder your statutes.

Psalm 119 (118): 43–8

BIBLE READING

Where is your wise man now, your man of learning, or your subtle debater – limited, all of them, to this passing age? God has made the wisdom of this world look foolish. As God in his wisdom ordained, the world failed to find him by its wisdom, and he chose to save those who have faith by the folly of the Gospel. Jews call for miracles, Greeks look for wisdom; but we proclaim Christ – yes, Christ nailed to the cross; and though this is a stumbling-block to Jews and folly to Greeks, yet to those who have heard his call, Jews and Greeks alike, he is the power of God and the wisdom of God.

1 Corinthians 1: 20–4

SECOND READING

Too often when we bring a message, people can perceive us and a message which, perhaps, comes through us, because we are not sufficiently identified with what we have to say. In order to be identified we must so read the Gospel, make it so much ourselves, and ourselves so much the Gospel, that when we speak from within it, in its name, it should be simply God's voice. The second thing is that to attain to that state . . . in which all that people could perceive of him was a man who had been completely transformed into a message, into a vision, into a proclamation, meant he was a man who consented to lay aside all that was selfish, grasping, all that was delighting selfishly in whatever he wanted to have. He had a pure heart, a clear mind, an unwavering will, a trained body, a complete mastery of self, so that when the message came, fear would not defeat him and make him silent; promises would not beguile him and keep him quiet, nor could the heaviness of the flesh, of the mind, of the heart, overcome the lightness and the lightening power of the Spirit.

Anthony Bloom, *God and Man*

PRAYERS

We pray for
  universities, colleges and schools
    those who seek for or proclaim the truth
    those who suffer for the sake of the truth

Almighty God,
you have enlightened your Church
  by the teaching of your servant N.
Enrich it evermore with your heavenly grace,
and raise up faithful witnesses,
who by their life and teaching
may proclaim to all men the truth of your salvation;
through Jesus Christ our Lord.

Our Father

Proclaim the message, press it home on all occasions, convenient or inconvenient, use argument, reproof, and appeal, with all the patience that the work of teaching requires.

Those in Religious Orders

All those things that I might count as profit I now reckon as loss, for Christ's sake.

Philippians 3: 7

PSALM

My part, I have resolved, O Lord,
is to obey your word.
With all my heart I implore your favour;
show the mercy of your promise.
I have pondered over my ways
and returned to your will.
I made haste and did not delay
to obey your commands.
At midnight I will rise and thank you
for your just decrees.

Psalm 119 (118): 57–60. 62

BIBLE READING

Jesus said, 'It is much harder for a rich man to enter the Kingdom of God than for a camel to go through the eye of a needle.' The people who heard him asked, 'Who, then, can be saved?' Jesus answered, 'What is impossible for men is possible for God.' Then Peter said, 'Look! We have left our homes to follow you.' 'Yes', Jesus said to them, 'and I tell you this: anyone who leaves home or wife or brothers or parents or children for the sake of the Kingdom of God will receive much more in this present age, and eternal life in the age to come'.

Luke 18: 25–30

The whole history of Monasticism is the emphasis of the importance of the conquest of self – in other words, of renunciation – as the one condition of effective work in the world. As we run through the record of the leaders that Monasticism produced, we discern clearly that they best will help to subjugate the world who have first obtained the victory in their own souls, that they are best fitted for work in the world who have succeeded in freeing themselves from its clasp. Not by coming down to lower levels, but by living on the mountain-tops, will men influence their fellows most powerfully. Throughout its career Monasticism utters its protest against the idea that an accommodated Christianity will ever influence the age to whose supposed needs it has been adapted.

H. B. Workman, *The Evolution of the Monastic Ideal*

PRAYERS

We give thanks for the life and witness of . . .

We pray for
   all religious communities, especially . . .
   all who seek to live under vows

Almighty God,
by whose grace N
kindled with the fire of your love,
became a burning and a shining light in the Church:
inflame us with the same spirit of discipline and love,
that we may ever walk before you as children of light;
through Jesus Christ our Lord.

Our Father

All these things that I might count as profit I now reckon as loss, for Christ's sake.

Any Saint

How blest are those whose hearts are pure; they shall see God.

Matthew 5: 8

PSALM

My song is of mercy and justice;
I sing to you, O Lord.
I will walk in the way of perfection.
O when, Lord, will you come?

I will walk with blameless heart
within my house;
I will not set before my eyes
whatever is base.

I will hate the ways of the crooked;
they shall not be my friends.
The false-hearted must keep far away;
the wicked I disown.

Psalm 101 (100): 1–4

BIBLE READING

Remember what you were, brothers, when God called you. Few of you were wise, or powerful, or of high social standing, from the human point of view. God purposely chose what the world considers nonsense in order to put wise men to shame, and what the world considers weak in order to put powerful men to shame. He chooses what the world looks down on, and despises, and thinks is nothing, in order to destroy what the world thinks is important. This means that no one can boast in God's presence. But God has brought you into union with Christ Jesus, and God has made Christ to be our wisdom; by him we are put right with God, we become God's holy people and are set free.

1 Corinthians 1: 26–30

Both in history and in life it is a phenomenon by no means rare to meet with comparatively unlettered people who seem to have struck profound spiritual depths and reached the real poetry of things – reached what I should regard as the very quintessence of the good life – while there are highly educated people of whom one feels that they are performing clever antics with their minds to cover a gaping hollowness that lies within. Some of the men who lived most fully and reflected on experience most profoundly would not bear comparison with an average English schoolboy today if we judged them by their book-learning and by their scientific knowledge – of which Jesus Christ himself must have had very little . . . Even in the study of history a kind of acquired simplicity is needed just to see things as they really are, just to see things naked, instead of envisaging them in the categories which historians have created to fit them into.

H. Butterfield, *Christianity and History*

PRAYERS

Gracious and holy Father,
give us wisdom to perceive you,
  diligence to seek you,
  patience to wait for you,
  eyes to behold you,
  a heart to meditate upon you,
  and a life to proclaim you;
  through the power of the Spirit
  of Jesus Christ our Lord.

St Benedict

Almighty God,
you have built up your Church
through the love and devotion of your saints.
We give thanks for your servant N
whom we commemorate today.
Inspire us to follow his/her example,
that we in our generation may rejoice with him/her
in the wisdom of your glory;
through Jesus Christ our Lord.

Our Father

How blest are those whose hearts are pure; they shall see God.

Thanksgiving for Baptism

By our own baptism, we were buried with him and shared his death, in order that, just as Christ was raised from death by the glorious power of the Father, so also we might live a new life.

Romans 6: 4

PSALM

I will bless the Lord continually:
his praise shall be always in my mouth.

Let my soul boast of the Lord:
the humble shall hear it and rejoice.

O praise the Lord with me:
let us exalt his name together.

For I sought the Lord's help and he answered:
and he freed me from all my fears.

Psalm 34 (33): 1–4

BIBLE READING

I will sprinkle clean water upon you, and you shall be clean from all your uncleannesses, and from all your idols I will cleanse you. A new heart I will give you, and a new spirit I will put within you: and I will take out of your flesh the heart of stone and give you a heart of flesh. And I will put my spirit within you, and cause you to walk in my statutes and be careful to observe my ordinances.

You shall dwell in the land which I gave to your fathers; and you shall be my people, and I will be your God.

Ezekiel 36: 25–8